FOLEY'S ASIA

in memoriam
Stafford Mary Adye-Curran RAMC

FOLEY'S ASIA

Ronan Sheehan

THE LILLIPUT PRESS
DUBLIN

First published 1999 by
THE LILLIPUT PRESS LTD
62-63 Sitric Road, Arbour Hill,
Dublin 7, Ireland.

A CIP record for this
title is available from
The British Library.

ISBN 1 901866 36 x

*The Lilliput Press receives financial assistance from
An Chomhairle Ealaíon/The Arts Council of Ireland.*

Set in 11.5 on 16 Janson with Copperplate display headings
Printed by ßetaprint, Clonshaugh, Dublin

FOLEY'S ASIA

ONE

VISIT THE ALBERT MEMORIAL in Hyde Park, London, these days and you'll find the entire construction, long neglected, restored by 'English Heritage' under the patronage of Prince Charles. Albert, the gigantic figure at the centre, was shaped and cast by the Dublin sculptor John Henry Foley, who likewise executed Asia, by common consent the must successful of the four groups of continents around the base of the memorial.

The commission for Albert was originally granted to Marochetti. The fashionable, well thought of, well connected, Paris-based, self-styled Italian baron.

The business got off to a bad start. He demanded £10,000 up front before he so much as made a sketch. No bronze figure of such size had ever been attempted before in London, so it was difficult to argue with him. But argument there was. He changed his position and said he'd kick off for £3000, which was maybe what he'd been angling for all the time.

Albert had to be sitting. He had to be fifteen feet, three inches tall on a base of ten feet, nine inches by nine feet. Marochetti had to produce two models. A smaller one for £1000. If Victoria approved this, it would be worked up into a full-size model to be tried for effect on the pedestal. For this he'd receive another £3000. But, as it happened, Marochetti's models did not meet with royal approval. The Baron died – the commission passed to Foley.

When complete, it had no fewer than 1500 parts. A colossal tribute to Victoria's consort, who is depicted sitting, thoughtful, holding a catalogue of the Great Exhibition. It is the archetypal icon of the Victorian age.

And what of Asia? The serene woman on the elephant with her magnificent torso, the shaping of which so obsessed Foley that he spent long hours astride the figure on wet clay, an experience which contributed to his catching the pleurisy from which he died. She is large, languid, sensuous, rich. There are jewels around her neck and arms, around her wrists, around her forehead. She lifts a veil from her face, which is calm and proud and beautiful. Her breasts are big and voluptuous. She feigns no interest in the doings of the busy British people behind her. Nor does the crouching elephant upon which she sits, with his curling trunk, wrinkled skin and mood of quiet, sullen potency.

Around the elephant are an Arab, an Indian, a Persian, a Chinese. None relates to one another, much less to the body of the memorial. In sculptural terms, this amounts to an act of subversion.

So, in Foley's contribution to the memorial, we find the double vision of the colonized artist. On the one hand he makes the grand icon of Albert at the centre of the memorial. On the other, he makes Asia, which undermines the entire process. Affirmation goes hand in hand with denial.

It is a mode of duality rather than a contradiction in terms. It expresses the emotion I feel for my grandfather, an Irishman who served in the army over which Victoria presided for so many years.

TWO

I WAS FOUR or five years old, playing on the kitchen floor while my mother ironed. I asked her to tell me a story about when she was young. So she told me about India.

She and her sister were playing hide and seek in the garden. Their ayah's attention was distracted by the sound of a younger child crying. They sneaked into the shrubbery and crawled along the ground until they came to the wall at the end of the garden. They climbed it and walked along the top until they left the territory of their own house and passed the gardens of their neighbours' houses. They reached a garden which contained a magnificent greenhouse, belonging to one Colonel Blenkinsop. The two girls were peering through the glass at the flowers, plants and fruit when suddenly! the stones beneath them moved, they lost their footing, and fell straight through

6

the roof of the Colonel's greenhouse. They were too terrified even to scream, because they ought not to have been there in the first place. Miraculously, they were unhurt. The Colonel's gardener Aziz arrived, having heard the crash, and threw a fit at the sight of the destruction. Now, doubly terrified, they fled, scrambling back up the wall, crawling frantically back along it until they reached their own garden where the ayah was crying out for her charges ... Trembling, they reached their bedroom, to await the return of their father. It was an age before he came, because an emergency case had come into the hospital minutes before he was due to leave and he had had to operate. He did not need two crises in one day. But he did not shout at them, or even get very cross. He checked that they were all right, examining their arms and legs for shards of glass. Then he instructed them to compose a letter of apology to Colonel Blenkinsop, which included a vow never to return to his wall upon their father's injunction. There and then they sat down and composed the letter. One of the houseboys took it around to the Colonel's. Father added a note of his own offering to pay compensation for the damage.

Once the letter was sent he relaxed. He told the ayah to put the girls to bed. He came up to their room soon afterwards and read them a story. Next morning, he called them for early mass. Together they knelt in the front pew and prayed that everything would be all right. The prayer was answered. At breakfast, the houseboy brought in a response from the Colonel. He forgave the girls – and said he would be satisfied with a contribution towards the cost of repairs. He invited the whole family to join his picnic group which was setting out for the hills after the parade.

They were to meet on the Maidan at 3 p.m. sharp … So that was the end to the story about Colonel Blenkinsop.

But it was not the end of the story about my grandfather. His photograph stood upon the mantelpiece in the dining-room. He had a kind, gentle face yet with a determined expression. When my mother or her sisters told me I looked like him I was pleased. He wore a military cap and a uniform. I knew he was a soldier – a doctor and a soldier. I did not know then of course that the uniform represented the British Empire, not our country. I knew that he was a Colonel – I knew that that meant he was of equal rank with Colonel Blenkinsop. I could not quite understand why he should have been so concerned about another Colonel. But the essential thing about him was that he was my grandfather. I loved him. Yet I could not say that I knew who he really was. He was dead. Long dead before I was born. And what he bequeathed to me, perhaps at the moment when I saw his photograph, or the moment when I was told that I resembled him, or the moment when the story about Colonel Blenkinsop finished, was an emotion which entered my heart, one which I could not name until many years afterwards. And so I

tried to imagine him through imagining his world, from scraps of information I collected from my mother and grandmother, from objects I saw lying about our house and our cousins' houses and my grandmother's house: the collection of brass animals he had brought home from India, the brass shellcasings he had gathered in France in 1918, the diaries he had written there which I was too young to read.

It was as though his spirituality, met through such objects and such stories, survived in his absence.

It was from that source that my fascination with Foley's statues was drawn, without my ever having heard of Foley. Their aspect connected with the part of my psyche which my grandfather had claimed.

THREE

IN DUBLIN, 'the Park' means the Phoenix Park. In a
city of parks, it's the Park. It's not just my favourite
park, but my favourite place here. If you want to
breathe, if you want to feel free, if you want to escape
the claustrophobia, the Park is where to go. Most places
in Dublin – in Ireland – are small. It's big, 1752 acres,
twice the size of Hyde Park and Regents Park put
together, the largest enclosed park in Europe. The best
approach is from south of the river, the way we went that
day, along Thomas Street. You pass the great old railway
station at Kingsbridge, cross the river and climb
Parkgate Street, with its redbrick row of shops and pubs.
Now you approach the enormous wrought-iron gates.
You see the gas-lamps along the tree-lined road which
runs dead straight to the Castleknock Gate, almost three
miles on.

Stephen turned right up Infirmary Road, then right again at the top, along the North Circular Road. The twisting of the car threw Rita and me up against one another.

He parked, bought three bottles of Chianti. Off again. He finally stopped on Baggot Road and we entered on foot through a gate there.

At the Zoological Gardens the cherry, crab and plum trees were all in flower, and many shrubs too, in yellow, red and purple. We drank our first wine beneath the great beech tree which Queen Victoria had planted beside the Reptile House. Stephen produced a packed lunch, chicken minestrone soup with Parmesan cheese.

Rita's dress slid up her thighs a little.

We reached the polo-ground halfway through the fourth chukker between Portobello and Fermanagh. Lord Waterford, perhaps the best player in the country, was number 4 for Portobello. A superb horseman. He dashed up and down the field on Khan who, with his small head, strong ribs and close-cropped tail, looked like a small steeplechaser. Rita took a shine to Waterford in his red vest and gaberdine breeches. He used a whippy cane with a cigar-shaped head for a stick, India style. There was a bit of needle between himself and Mr Fennell, playing back for Fermanagh. Fennell used a Malacca. He would hook Waterford from time to time when the umpire was unsighted. He had an excellent positional sense and was a first-class backhand striker. But Waterford was great at nursing the ball right up to him, then riding out. Khan was superior to Fennell's mount. He could play the game himself, stop in his own length, turn on a sixpence. The goal Waterford scored just after the bell, from twenty-five yards or so, came when Khan created space by veering left and stopping dead, while Fennell sputtered on. He cantered near us, his right arm raised. We sat up and cheered and he waved to us.

Stephen led us to the main road, where we saw another horse, this one made of bronze.

It was a formidable piece of work, the pedestal six feet and the horse and rider twice that. GOUGH was written on one side and on the other the following words:

In honour of Field-Marshal Hugh Viscount Gough K.P.G.C.B.C.S.I. An illustrious Irishman whose achievement in the Peninsular War, in China, and in India, have added lustre to the military glory of this country, which he faithfully served for 75 years. This statue (cast from the cannon taken by troops under his command and granted by parliament for the purpose) is erected by his friends and comrades.

I could almost sense the energy of a real horse from this one. The hind legs and the left foreleg were set firmly on the ground, while his right foreleg was arched in the air, caught in the act of stepping forward. His neck too was arched and his mouth pulled in almost to his shoulders: a horse to a tight rein, controlled for the parade ground or march-past. The tail swished impatiently against the right buttock. The rider's back, by contrast, was ramrod straight. In his left hand he held the rein and in his right a baton, at arm's length, to give the impression that he was balancing in the saddle. This impression was developed by the way the feet were stuck in the stirrups, toes pointing up and out, balls of the feet on the bar, heels low and inward.

The riding boots came up to his thighs. There were tassels, embroidery and different decorations on the front of his jacket – the uniform of a Colonel of the Blues. His expression held nothing of the haughtiness you might have expected from a Field-Marshal. There was sternness, certainly, but this was softened by something sad in his eyes. He had a moustache, long sideburns and wavy hair receding from a big forehead. He looked a good sixty years of age, a silver-haired grandfather.

Gough Statue Dublin

I closed my eyes and imagined Gough leaping from the pedestal and cantering towards the polo-ground to join the game.

We drifted to the cricket pitch on the south side of the road, where the fielders seemed much younger than the batsmen: Trinity were playing Phoenix. Stephen soon tired of it. He went off by himself to study for the umpteenth time the tableaux upon the enormous obelisk which commemorates the Duke of Wellington.

13

I sneaked my arm around Rita's waist. She bit me – well, nipped me – on the neck.

Hours later, in the pitch dark, we rendezvoused with Stephen. He gave us each a whistle. We went separate ways, she to watch the police depot near the zoo, while I watched the main road. Stephen climbed the equestrian statue. He opened his attaché case and pulled out of it what from my angle seemed like a collection of tin cans and pieces of string. He set one at the horse's neck, another at its foreleg, another at the rider's throat and so on. He placed the case between the horse's hind legs. Then he jumped to the ground and ran to the bushes at the side of the road, where he sounded his whistle. We all ran together to the North Circular Road gate, where he ordered us to lie flat.

The explosion was loud, terrifying. There was a flash of light. I thought the wall of the Park was going to fall on me. We heard the sound of falling metal and splintering wood. Stephen pulled us to our feet. We ran through the gate and there, on Infirmary Road, was an Anglia, engine running. In twenty minutes we were sitting in a house in Chapelizod, drinking Chianti and eating tagliatelli done in pesto sauce.

FOUR

Barossa, Spain, 1811

I
T'S THE FAULT of La Peña, the wretched Spanish
general.

The object of the exercise is to secure communication
across the Santi Petri river. La Peña has ordered Graham,
the British general, to march from the low ridge of
Barossa to the Torre Bermeja, which is about halfway up
the river, there to effect a junction with himself. Graham
doubts the wisdom of this manoeuvre, believing the key
to the whole position to be the height of Barossa – any
attack upon Bermeja would leave a flank exposed to that
quarter. Having ordered Colonel Brown to occupy the
height with a rearguard, he sets off. Halfway there – one
mile's march – he learns that the French are pouring out
of the woods in strength, making for the ridge.

Graham changes direction. But before he clears the

woods, Maréchal Victor drives Brown from the height. Since La Peña is nowhere to be seen, Graham has no option but to attack.

Hugh Gough leads the 87th from the woods. He forms a line, throws out his flank in view of the enemy's advance. They must await their moment, exposed to appalling fire. A major, a captain, two lieutenants and fifty men fall. Then the French guns are silent.

'*Faugh a beallagh!*' Gough cries. '*Faugh a beallagh!*' 'Clear the way!'

The Irish surge forward. At twenty-five yards the Grenadiers break ranks. Since they were standing in column, they cannot escape. They are at the mercy of the 87th. No defence is offered for a quarter of an hour. Hundreds of French throats, stomachs and hearts are ripped apart by the bayonets of the Irishmen.

Ensign Keogh spots the eagle, of well-gilt brass, with its laurel wreath of gold (a gift from Napoleon). He lunges for it, gets his hands on the poll, then is struck down dead. Sergeant Patrick Masterson drives his sword through the French officer who holds it. He grabs the eagle himself and never lets it go for the rest of the day. But there's trouble coming.

Maréchal Laval's 47th division appears on the scene. Gough's men have marched sixteen hours before the battle. How can they meet the onslaught of fresh troops? He has to rally them. He has to batter them from their victims.

'*Eirigi! Eirigi!*' he roars. 'Rise up!'

Exhausted, blood-gorged, frenzied, they must charge for their lives. The battle cry sounds again. The 87th staggers forward, firing, firing. At fifty yards the 47th breaks ranks and flies.

The Duke of Wellington presents the eagle, the first eagle taken in the war, to the Prince Regent. His Majesty is so delighted that he awards the title 'The Prince of Wales Own Irish Regiment' to the Faugh-a-Beallaghs. Their next action is at the port of Tarifa. Victor and Laval make siege to it with ten thousand men. The big French guns open a breach to the right of the portcullis. At 8 a.m., on the last day of the year, two thousand Grenadiers advance. Gough orders the band to play 'Garryowen':

> *We are the boys that take delight in*
> *Smashing the Limerick lamps when lighting,*
> *Through the streets like sporters fighting*
> *And tearing all before us.*
> *We'll break windows, we'll break doors,*
> *The watch knock down by threes and fours,*
> *Then let the doctors work their cures*
> *And tinker up our bruises.*
>
> *Instead of spa we'll drink brown-ale*
> *And pay the reckoning on the nail,*
> *No man for debt shall go to jail*
> *From Garryowen in glory!*

The 87th lets rip with a ferocious fusillade. It overwhelms Laval's men. They're ordered back from the breach. Then, suddenly, forward again to the portcullis. Now Gough has the band play 'St Patrick's Day':

> *Oh! Blest be the days when the green banner floated*
> *Sublime o'er the mountains of free Inisfail*
> *Her sons to her glory and freedom devoted*
> *Defied the invader to tread her soil.*

When back o'er the main they chased the Dane
And gave to religion and learning their spoil;
When valour and mind together combined –

But wherefore lament o'er the glories departed?
Her star shall shine out with as vivid a ray,
For ne'er had she children so brave and true-hearted
As those she now sees on St Patrick's Day!

Once more their fire is deadly. Once more the Grenadiers are scythed down. The plucky French commander collapses against the bars and passes his sword through to Gough. Laval reckons it's not worth the effort anymore and retires.

For Gough, the Grand Cross of the Order of Charles III of Spain. For the 87th, a glowing report from General Ross, a welcome antidote to the carpers who say the regiment is only good for wild charges in an hour of excitement.

At Victoria, Gough is hit in three places and has a horse killed under him. The 87th delivers a smack to the puss of their long-standing foe Jourdan, making off with his baton, a velvet embroidered affair with gold eagles at either end which winds up in the hands of the Prince Regent.

After the war, Gough retires to a farm in Tipperary on a pension of £330 p.a. His wounds slowly heal. To his dismay, despite the eagle and the baton, the Prince Regent makes no concessions to Catholics. Throughout the south of Ireland, the Whiteboys conduct a campaign of burning crops, maiming cattle, turning over land, murder. Gough leads a Protestant regiment against them in North Cork and Tipperary.

Gough's years of retirement end in 1837, with an appointment to the command of the Mysore Division of the Madras army. But the scene of his next campaign lies farther to the east, in China, where the authorities have seized the stocks of British opium sellers in an effort to suppress the supply of the drug to their people. British traders appeal to their government.

On the 24th of May 1841, Victoria's twenty-second birthday, Gough's troops land on Chinese soil. They advance on Canton. A bombardment drives defenders from the western forts. Both these and the eastern forts are now attacked by some four thousand Chinese who occupy rising-ground to the north-east of the city. Gough leads the 18th Royal Irish and Her Majesty's 49th along a narrow causeway to the camp from which, after a brief, fierce engagement, they drive out the Chinese and explode their magazines. Next morning the white flag flies over Canton, but the officer in command fails to turn up to meet Gough to discuss terms. Rain delays the assault for a further twenty-four hours. Then, just as he is about to take the city, the Limerickman is furious to discover that the battle is off. The Chinese had made a deal over his head. The chief condition is that $6,000,000 must be paid in one week.

Months of tedious negotiations follow, while Gough counsels the rapid advancement of the war. Military might is what commands respect from the Chinese. Pauses only afford them an opportunity to use guile. He wants to move up the Yang-Tse-Kiang river to attack Nanking. At length the British government tires of diplomacy. Sir Henry Pottinger arrives on the scene, together with Rear-Admiral Sir William Parker.

At Amoy, whose citizens reject the Admiral's summons to surrender, they have ninety-six big guns and enormous ramparts. But the Royal Irish and the 49th scale the walls and scatter the defenders. The citizens panic – they've never seen Europeans before. When the troops enter the inner-city, many Chinese commit suicide. The town is well and truly sacked.

At Tinghai, the Royal Irish leads the charge, bayoneting defenders along the wall of the city until they reach Pagoda Hill. Having planted the colours, they enter the city.

The Chinese arms are bad. Having stood for a while, they give way to our rush, and are then shot like hares in all directions. The slaughter of fugitives is unpleasant, but we are such a handful in the face of so wide a country and so large a force, that we should be swept away if we did not read our enemy a sharp lesson whenever we came in contact.

Slaughter ensues.

At Ningpo, the citizens open their gates without a struggle, thereby stymieing Pottinger's object of plundering the town as a punishment for resistance. He proposes instead to seize public and ransom private property. Gough demurs, declining to disperse his men 'to punish one set of robbers for the benefit of another set'.

At Chapoo, stiffest resistance is offered by the Tartars, many of whom, preferring death to the dishonour of defeat, destroy their wives, their children and themselves. Shanghai fell without a fight. On to Chingakingfoo, where again the Tartars fiercely resist, where again they kill themselves in defeat. At Nanking, Pottinger offers to spare the city on payment of a ransom. The Tartars refuse to accept these terms, so Gough prepares to bombard them into submission. But emissaries arrive from the Emperor, suing for peace. They agree to indemnify the opium-sellers and make a present of Hong-Kong to the British, among various other concessions.

Congratulations flood in. Wellington sends Gough a personal message and he's made a baronet. Parliament and the East India Company vote thanks.

A very different reaction greets his victory at Mahraj-pore the following year. Gough loses 790 killed and wounded in crushing the insolent Maharattas. Ellen-borough, the Governor-General of India, and the non-military set around him, complain these numbers are too high. They say Gough is obsessed by infantry charges and the bayonet. He thinks he's still fighting the Peninsular War. Why had he sent back his heavy guns? It doesn't come out until much later that Lady Gough and her daughter Frances were nearly counted among the casual-ties, when the elephants upon which they were watching proceedings drew enemy fire and bolted.

Gough takes the criticism in his stride. 'I never have been bate,' he observes. 'And I never will be bate.'

He comes very close to being bate at Ferozeshah in the First Sikh War. Tej Singh's troops arrive late to confront the exhausted British, who have not a shot left in their guns. Gough himself rushes forward to draw enemy fire from his infantry. Then a sunstruck officer of H.Q. staff, clad only in pyjamas, appears from nowhere to order the main body of cavalry and artillery back to Ferozepur. The sight of this lunatic manoeuvre renders Gough speechless with rage. But Tej Singh thinks it is a tactic designed to cut off his retreat, and retreats.

Should Gough have waited for General Littler's reinforcements to arrive before engaging the enemy? Sir Charles Gough later compared his uncle's position to that of Moltkë at Koniggratz:

> *Instead of waiting for a junction to be completed, he attacked the Austrians; the second army coming up and attacking the enemy in flank during the engagement – thus ensuring a decisive victory.*

The public fail to draw the analogy, concentrating instead upon the British dead: 215 at Moodkee, 694 at Ferozeshah, 320 in the final encounter at Sobraon. Gough's staff argue that this amounts to less than 15 per cent of the number of men involved. Marlborough lost 23 per cent at Blenheim, Wellington 25 per cent at Talavera. Journalists prove unconvinced by the comparison, uninterested in the scale of the casualties Gough had inflicted. They accuse him of being unable to control his Irish blood, 'Tipperary tactics'. They mock his brogue.

This is minor carping, compared to the torrent of abuse prompted a couple of years later by the battle of Chillianwallah in the Second Sikh War. Gough loses 2338 killed or wounded. They say he has no soldierly quality except brute courage. According to some he had made no preparations. Everyone agrees he had flown into a rage the moment his men came under fire.

'I'll wipe de Sakes off de face of de earth,' he is quoted as saying.

He acts too quickly. He acts too slowly. He knows nothing of the basic principles of warfare. He is too excitable. Indeed, he is a maniac. He is a monstrous composite of folly and inhumanity. He is a reckless Irish savage whose command of the army is bound to result in the loss of an empire.

> *Chillianwallah, Chillianwallah,*
> *'Tis a village dark and low,*
> *By the bloody Jhelum river*
> *Bridged by the foreboding foe.*
> *And across the wintry water*
> *He is ready to retreat,*
> *When the carnage and the slaughter*
> *Shall have paid for his defeat.*
>
> *Chillianwallah, Chillianwallah,*
> *When the night set in with rain*
> *Came the savage, plundering devils*
> *To their work among the slain.*
> *And the wounded and the dying*
> *In cold blood did share the doom*
> *Of their comrades round them lying*
> *Stiff in the dead skyless gloom.*

On to Gujerat, Gough tempting Shere Singh to a position between the fortress and a ford on the Chenab river above Wazirabad. A 'wonderfully calm and fair morning'. Gough rides the line in his white fighting coat, to tumultuous cheers. The British advance at seven thirty and the Sikhs fire immediately, revealing the position of their guns. The British reply with a devastating bombardment lasting two and a half hours. At noon, Gough orders a general advance. His light troops encounter tremendous fire from the village of Burra Kalra, which they had thought deserted. The First Europeans (later the Dublin Fusiliers) suffer severe losses in taking the position. At the village of Chota Kalra, a large force of Sikh cavalry and infantry compel General Hervey to give way. The Sikhs threaten to pour through the gap created, but Whisp fills it. By one o'clock the British have the town of Gujerat, the Sikh camp, their baggage and artillery. The cavalry is in full pursuit on both flanks. It's a complete and total rout, Gough's last and greatest victory, his vindication.

The Punjab is annexed.

The government awards a pension of £2000 p.a. to Gough and his next two heirs. The East India Company awards another pension. He's granted the freedom of the city of London, made a Viscount. The Duke of Wellington declares that Hugh Gough has 'himself afforded the brightest example of the highest qualities of the British soldier in the attainment of the glorious successes which have attended the British army under his command'.

Gough retires to Dublin, where each succeeding year brings new honours. His homes at St Helen's in Booterstown and Lough Cutra in Galway become places of pilgrimage for the military set. In 1863 his beloved Frances dies. Victoria's personal message of sympathy recalls her having met Frances in the Phoenix Park in 1853 and 'how kind and amiable' she was. In 1869 the old soldier himself dies at St Helen's, Booterstown, aged ninety, to be buried beside Frances in St Bridgid's graveyard, Stillorgan. An inscription on his tomb shares the glory of his campaigns with the Great Commanding Officer:

Oh Lord
Thou strength of my breath,
Thou hast carried my head in the day of battle.

Dublin Corporation commissions Foley to make an equestrian statue. Claiming to be affected by the general outbreak of patriotism, Foley agrees to do the work for 'half the normal fee'. On February the 21st, 1880 (the thirty-first anniversary of Gujerat), the statue is unveiled by the Viceroy, the Duke of Marlborough. General Sir John Michel, commanding the forces in Ireland, encourages the young troops present to look to Gough for their example and inspiration:

Honoured I have been by the temporary deposit in my hands of this memorial of glory. I now surrender it to the safe-guard of Ireland's sons. Keep it, Irishmen, as an everlasting memento of your glory. Treasure it as a sacred deposit. Glory in it as the statue of one who was an honour to your country, one whose whole life, whether civil or military, was one continued career of kindness, honour, honesty of purpose, combined with the purest loyalty and the most enthusiastic patriotism. He was loved and honoured by his countrymen. He was par excellence *our Irish chevalier,* sans peur et sans reproche, *and to wind up all, he was the heart and soul of an Irishman.*

FIVE

Nicholson Memorial, Lisburn Cathedral

I
T'S A FRIEZE, or tableau. An image first of a heap of
dead bodies – soldiers' bodies – on a wall. The wall of
a fortress. At bottom left, someone climbs a ladder. At
right, a party of soldiers, in formation, advances along the
wall with fixed bayonets. At left, a soldier lies on his
elbow, a pistol in his right hand, waving the others on
with his hat which he holds in his left hand. There is a
flag planted among the bodies. There is a Union Jack at
the top left hand. Beneath the image, this inscription:

*The Grave of Brigadier-General John Nicholson, C.B., is
beneath the fortress he died to take. This monument is
erected by his mother to keep alive his memory and example among his countrymen. Comrades who loved and
mourn him add the story of his life ... Rare gifts had
marked him out for great things in peace and war. He*

had an iron mind and frame, a terrible courage, an indomitable will. His form seemed made for an army to behold: his heart, to meet the crisis of an empire ... Soldier and civilian, he was a tower of strength: the type of the conquering race ...

14 September 1857, Delhi
The first day of the assault drew to a close. John Nicholson, shot through the lung and abandoned by his stretcher-bearers, was found beneath the Kashmir Gate. They carried him to a field hospital, where a surgeon administered morphine.

The pain vanished.

The outlines of people and objects surrounding him merged. All colours in his vision became one: blue.

He sees a figure wearing a great cloak and top-hat, carrying a leather bag. Alexander Nicholson, Assistant Physician at the Lying-In Hospital, Mercer Street, Dublin. He is walking home through St Stephen's Green on a winter evening. The crisp blue January sky is turning grey. A film of frost covers the grass and flower beds. The trees are damp and bare.

A granite pedestal as tall as a tree stands in the centre of the Green. Upon it there is a great bronze horse. George II of Great Britain and Ireland, decked out like a Roman Emperor, sits in the saddle. Four boys stage a cavalry battle around the base of the monument. Alexander sits on John's shoulders, William perches on Charles.

They advance, and retreat, seriously now that their father is watching.

'*Cavalerie, chargez!*' says Charles.

'*La Garde recule,*' says John.

The physician leads his little platoon back to barracks, No. 35 Dawson Street, where Mother waits at the dining-room table. She is smiling. The Bible is open in her lap. 'Ye are the sons of Israel,' she says, 'ye shall drive the nations before ye …'

John looks around the table, His brothers are still and pale. His sisters are weeping. Mother and Father are missing.

He climbs three flights of stairs to the top of the house, pushes open a door. Father lies on the bed, dead. His hair is neatly combed. The lids are firmly shut upon his blue-grey eyes. His arms are crossed upon his breast. The marks of his boots and socks are visible upon his ankles. The cheeks are pink, warm.

As if waiting for him to put them on again, his clothes are stacked on two chairs. The black leather ankle boots. The plaid trousers and jacket. The cotton shirt with detachable cuffs and collar.

'Father, Father, are you there?'

Tears well up in his eyes, his muscles stiffen. His gaze wanders around the room. It rests upon the window. Mother forgot to close the shutters, although it's night. The night sky turns a deep blue. The rooftops of Dawson Street are missing.

He sees the snowcapped peaks of the mountains around Ghazni, Afghanistan. The garrison has surrendered. The sobbing of the bereaved Nicholson family of Dawson Street becomes the cries of his fellow officers, being tortured.

The feet of one are bound and stuck between the split side of a piece of wood which has been half buried in the ground. Another piece of wood lies on top of the feet. An Afghan strikes this with a heavier piece of wood. A second officer has his head thrust into the nosebag of a horse, in which tobacco or sulphur is smouldering. A third has a thin rope bound around his thigh, fastened to a long stick, twisted by two men.

'*Bin-e-Israneel*!' the Afghans say. 'We are the sons of Israel.'

A fourth officer has had an animal's intestine thrust into his own. An Afghan is blowing into it, making it swell.

'*Shumau moolk e mau mee geered?*' 'You will take my country?'

Their tormentors have dark skins and bushy eyebrows, twinkling brown eyes and beautiful white teeth. Their beards are black and curly. Their headdresses are made from Kashmir shawls. Their coats are sheepskins turned inside out, leather embroidered with blue, gold, orange and crimson silk threads.

Sad messages are scrawled upon the dungeon walls:

'AVENGE US!'
'Thomas Ward, Llanelly, died here January 1841'
'Lord God, help us in our hour of need.'

The dungeon vanishes. Nicholson sees instead a room in Kabul.

The floor is covered with thick Turkish carpets upon which satin mattresses are arranged each with a muslin pillow. Tallow candles, half as tall as a man, stand beside the walls, their smoke scenting of crushed jasmine.

The Afghans wash their hands in bowls of rosewater and sprinkle their beards with it. They dry their fingers in the curling black locks of boy servants.

Sherbets are produced in china dishes. There is raisin, orange and pomegranate juice. Sultan Jan, the handsomest man Nicholson has ever seen, slits a musk melon with his knife, and offers half. The fruit becomes liquid in his mouth, instantly dissolving. Lamb kebabs wrapped in vine leaves are brought in, with curries and vegetables, rice and apricots.

A lyre strikes up, then a trumpet, a horn, a drum. Girls glide between the mattresses. Their hair is plaited in tiny folds. Golden almonds hang from their ears and they have gold rings on their fingers. Their eyelashes are tinted, their arms and fingers henna-dyed. Their cheeks are rouged. They wear tiny chintz jackets and velvet trousers. Sometimes, when there is a pause in the music, they pluck a morsel from a dish to cram into the mouth of a favourite.

Sultan Jan disappears. The music fades. The dancing girls turn into the soldiers of General Nott's army, quitting Afghanistan.

At the mouth of the Khyber Pass, some distance from the line of the march, a body lies on a rock, naked and white. The fringe of fair hair is matted with blood from a cut across the forehead. The eyelashes are as long as a girl's and part of the right one has been blown away. The nose, lips and cheekbones are blue from the chill of the rock. The shoulders are lean. The groin has been hacked off. It's Alexander Nicholson, late of Dawson Street, Dublin, sixteen years.

On both sides of the gloomy defiles which wind through the mountains, the rock rises black, damp and sheer. In the spots where sunlight penetrates, stunted palm trees, wasted olives.

A silent army guards the ravines.

Their skeletons clog the paths. Cannon and carriage wheels grind their bones to powder. Their bones choke the mouths of caves in the cliff face. They are piled together in great heaps and mounds. In the darkest ravines and passages, the freezing cold has preserved their skin like leather, preserved their hair and features.

The living recognize their friends among the dead, cut locks of hair from their heads as mementos, little pieces of cloth.

'Take us with you,' they plead. 'We waited here for you. Now we want to be brought home.'

The living army vanishes and the dead.

Nicholson sees a man walking through a garden. He moves from a cluster of rose bushes to a row of mulberry trees. An African bee-eater, green and gold, rises from a clump of sweetbriar and hums around his turban. He has brilliant eyes, brown and green, dark skin, jet-black hair. Golab Singh, the Rajah of Jammu and Kashmir.

Who has not heard of the Vale of Kashmir,
Its roses the brightest that earth ever gave,
Its temples and fountains and grottoes as clear
As the lovelighted eyes that hang over their wave?

He comes forward.

'Captain Nicholson! My cook tried to poison me! He is dying at the present time. I separated his skin behind the neck, to the throat, then had the head flayed. Then I had the skin pulled over the skull.'

The roses are indifferent to the sufferings of the cook. Purple or red, white or yellow, their blossoms are as pure and their scent as fresh after they have heard of his fate as before.

Golab Singh leaves the garden through the doorway of a house.

Nicholson sees a house at Sakkar. It's a two-storey wooden house, set apart from the barracks compound, its shutters closed and front door locked. Monkeys gambol on the roof. In front of the verandah, the fruit of a pomegranate tree lies rotting on the ground.

Inside, there's a smell of burnt curry. The heat is overwhelming. In seconds, he's drenched in perspiration. He climbs two flights of stairs, gasping for breath. The bedroom door is open. Now he's standing in the room where William Nicholson died, aged twenty. The sheets are still on the bed.

We found him in bed, delirious. Two ribs broken. Multiple bruising on his head and body. He must have sleepwalked and fallen from the verandah, then crawled back up the stairs to bed.

But there's a railing around the verandah four feet high, and William was not much above five and a half feet. The drop to the ground is only fourteen feet. If what they say is true, why do the natives call the house the murder house? Why will no one live here?

Nicholson sees a stream. Cool, clear, gurgling water. Peacocks stalk the grass on either side, in the shade of acacia and jujube trees. This is where he camps to mourn William. He calls it 'The Bendemeer'.

There's a bower of roses by Bendemeer's stream
And the nightingale sings round it all the day long,
In the time of my childhood 'twas like a sweet dream
To sit in the roses and hear the birds' song.
The bower and its roses I never forget
But oft when alone in the bloom of the year
I think is the nightingale singing there yet
Are the roses still bright by the calm Bendemeer?
By the calm Bendemeer? By the calm Bendemeer?

No the roses soon withered that hung o'er the wave
But some blossoms were gather'd while freshly they shone,
And a dew was distilled from their flowers that gave
The fragrance of summer when summer was gone.

The colour of the water changes. The Bendemeer becomes the Indus. Nicholson glides downstream towards Bombay with his true friend, Captain Herbert Edwardes, whose curling blond hair falls across his forehead in a manner that recalls Alexander. He has brown eyes, pink cheeks, full lips.

Nicholson realizes that he loves Edwardes more than any of his brothers.

He sees the barracks square at Peshawar. A May morning. Edwardes has lined up the Sepoy regiments which together they had disarmed once news of the outbreak of mutiny came through from Naushera. The natives are tense, expectant.

Nicholson has rounded up 150 mutineers. They are starving and exhausted, many trying to staunch seeping wounds. Some look quizzically in the direction of their former comrades in arms. No one speaks.

Edwardes stands beside a row of ten cannon. He signals to Nicholson to send the first batch of prisoners forward.

Ten are marched up to the cannon and tied down, their stomachs against the mouths the guns. One by one the ten are blown away.

Then another ten.

Then another ten.

Then another ten.

There's total silence. No one moves. The natives have turned to ice.

Nicholson orders the other prisoners to collect the blasted pieces of flesh and bone.

Nicholson feels his body racked with pain. He can scarcely breathe. Breathing makes the pain worse. He's back in the field hospital outside Delhi. He hears a voice he recognizes call:

'John! John! Are you alive?'

Lying on the next bed is his brother, Charles. His right arm has been amputated.

'I'm dying,' Nicholson replies.

SIX

Sir Henry Lawrence
The Residence, Lucknow,
Oudh, India

30th June 1857

Alick Lawrence
Rugby School, Warwickshire
England

M

Y DEAR BOY,
The situation is grim here. The revolt of the native troops
has spread to this province of Oudh. We are under siege.
Some days ago a shell struck my room in the Residence
and caused me injury.

I foresaw the situation some weeks ago and made preparations. In May I disarmed the 7th Oudh Infantry, then pardoned all except those a court of enquiry found seriously guilty. All the European troops I could muster I have gathered within the walls of the city. I established the sick, women and children in the Residence. I laid in great stores of supplies, food, water and ammunition.

There can be no surrender. I saw at first hand the fate of those who surrendered at Kabul and Ghazni. It is anyway impossible to move all the white people out of this place. Retreat would undermine morale throughout the whole of India. I increased the pay of irregular soldiers so that we might maintain an alternative native soldiery when the regulars revolted. The policy paid off. One of them informed me of the date set for the outbreak and so enabled me to forewarn the European troops and prevent a massacre. We drove the rebels out of the town and took many prisoners.

Other outposts in the province collapsed. Cawnpore was the scene of a bloody massacre. Now the mutineers are concentrating here.

Apart from the Sepoys, my biggest problem is an insane little accountant named Martin Gubbins who thinks he knows best how to run things. Like many a man who has mastered one field of activity, he is straining at the bit to control other areas of which he knows nothing. In the collection and organisation of supplies he was invaluable. He suffers from the delusion that he is just as capable in the area of military intelligence. He spreads half his time dreaming up mad schemes for raiding the rebels and the other half trying to convince me of their merit. A couple of weeks ago he wanted to lead a team of volunteers some fifty miles away, on elephants, to blow up a munition dump.

Whenever I turned him down he would say, 'Sir Henry, we shall be branded cowards at the bar of history,' or words to that effect. Foolishly, I let his needling get under my skin. He saved up his worst barb for a few days ago.

'You are a Derry man, Sir Henry,' he said, all shifty smiles.

'Yes,' I replied. 'My family have been there for many generations. I was educated at Foyle College.'

'Do you know something about the great siege of Derry in 1689?'

'Every Foyle man knows the siege. What of it?'

'The besieged outnumbered the besiegers. Yet they did not break out upon them. They hadn't got the guts.'

This tallied with what my uncle Jimmy Knox had taught us at Foyle. There had been no out-break. But not from want of guts.

'The advance of Sepoys is gathering at Nawabganj,' he continued. 'Now is the time to strike them. At present they number only 500 or so.'

The implication of his words was clear enough. If I did not sally out now, I was as much a coward as my ancestors who cringed within the walls in 1689. The gibe prompted me to make the worst military mistake of my career.

I organized a force consisting of some 300 European and 230 native troops, plus 100 Sikh horses. We brought four light guns and a howitzer. The heat that day was unbearable. When we reached Kukpail I discovered that the native contingent in charge of food and supplies had deserted. There was nothing for the men to drink. They were thirsty, exhausted and generally miserable. We could and should have turned back at that point. Gubbins brought in some native travellers who said that Chinhat, a few miles farther on, was empty. He advised that we advance there for the purpose of surveying the situation ourselves. I ordered the troops to march. It transpired that the native travellers had been lying and that Gubbins' estimate of the enemy's strength was wildly out. The enemy was waiting for us at Chinhat, in ten times the strength Gubbins had declared. They handled themselves effectively, concentrating fire on the Europeans, beginning an encircling movement. Our reserve gunners deserted. We had no choice but to withdraw. The truth is that our retreat quickly became a rout. For five minutes or so I attempted to rally the men at Kukpail Bridge. We lost 200 dead in all. Half the Europeans were killed or wounded. We lost the light guns and the howitzer. The siege began immediately – we might have had more days to prepare. In short, we were ten times worse off than we had been before we set out.

I wish I could hang Gubbins.

Alick, should you ever be so misfortunate as to find yourself in command of a besieged garrison, follow the example of the Apprentice Boys of Derry rather than your father. Shut the gates and hang on.

My room here on the top-floor is exposed but is the best position from which to conduct the defence. Ironically, it was a shell from the howitzer they captured from us which hit it. Your cousin George was with me. It was a miracle that we survived. Officers begged me to quit the room for safer quarters. I refused.

'I don't think they've anyone good enough to put another shot into this little room, have they?' I said.*

---

* A fatal error of judgment on Sir Henry's part. The shot which killed him entered the self-same room at 8.30 a.m. on July the 2nd.

The thing is, I shouldn't be here at all. I should be in the Punjab. But I was given the heave-ho out of that province to which I had devoted the best years of my life by a certain Governor-General, an arrogant Scottish aristocrat. He demoted me in favour of my brother John. Everyone knew that the successful administration of that province was the fruit of my work and my methods. I was the Punjab. Lord Hardinge recognized my achievement and was content to let me get on with it, in my own way with my own team. But he was succeeded by Dalhousie who was obsessed by rank, being master in his own house, wanting all the kudos himself. Myself, John and Robert Montgomery – all Foyle College old boys! – formed the Punjab Board which ruled the province after the Second Sikh War. The others accepted that I was the chief since I had been sole ruler in all but name before the war. True, there were disagreements between John and myself, but no more than you would expect in any government charged with rule of so many millions in so vast a territory. Dalhousie seized on these to challenge the structure of the administration. He put me in a position which left me no alternative but to offer my resignation. He promptly accepted it. And I realized this was what he'd been angling for all along. As you know, I was sent to darkest Rajputana. Then here to Oudh, when Dalhousie annexed the province (in breach of the terms of the treaty).

I am convinced this is what killed your mother. She was heartbroken to see me banished from the province I loved and in which I was revered.

Marry a Donegal woman when the time comes. They are intelligent, hardy, practical, fiercely determined and can travel up-country for long distances. They are loyal and not afraid of a fight. Your mother was a prime example of the breed. I remember well our first meetings. I was returned to Ireland after the expedition into Burma. Like so many others, I had caught the fever there. I was weak. I had little money and my prospects were distant to say the least. My father was dead and we boys tried to put by a percentage of our pay for our mother and the rest of the family. It was my sister who brought Honoria Marshall to our house. Then I visited her at her father's home in Carndonagh, County Donegal, and afterwards at Lough Fahan on the Inishowen peninsula in that county, where her aunt lived.

What a spirit she had! What a beauty!

She understood that I was not then in a position to ask her to be my wife. I returned to India. She waited for me for five years. We next met in London. It was in the spring of 1828. I remember the time well for that was the first occasion on which we walked out together. I escorted her to a shoe-market. Our path took us to St Paul's Cathedral. Your mother said she was very disappointed by it. There was nothing grand about it. We spent an age looking at it, inside and out. We wandered through the neighbourhood around the Cathedral and your mother was shocked and moved to tears by the foul conditions in which the poor of the city lived.

At that time the army was conducting the Trigonometric Survey in County Donegal, the first of its kind. It was your mother who drew my attention to this. I applied for, obtained permission to work with it. Thus I gained the experience which afterwards entitled me to survey the North-West Provinces. While the primary considerations were military, I quickly grasped that the work afforded unrivalled possibilities for studying the language, customs and economy of the native population. What I learned in Donegal, I applied in India.

I agree with the estimate of my friends who said it was the Survey, plus your mother, which made me. To me now, the two seem indivisible.

The position I obtained on the survey in India gave me a salary which entitled me to ask for your mother's hand in marriage. She came out and for many years we lived in the countryside while the work endured. I normally had two or three assistants, twelve clerks and many dozens of natives. The natives measured each field with a chain and mapped out a region with the eye. They compiled a statement of the size of each field, its soil and crop. I and my assistants mapped the same area with theodolites and other instruments. The two maps were then compared and a separate one made on the basis of both. We also gathered information about the population, the number of houses, the castles to which the people belonged. So many maps made up one 'volume', copies of which were provided to the Collector and to the Governor-General. Upon this basis the revenue of the various regions was assessed and upon the revenue the whole administration naturally depended.

My knowledge of the Indian farmer, and my sympathy for him, were developed in those years in a unique fashion. I was trusted. Then, although a white man, I came to be seen as a kind of leader.

Your mother encouraged and guided me in everything. She cheerfully bore the hardships of the camp. Indeed, she delighted in meeting the demands of her new way of life. I have one image of her which stands out from the rest. A visitor arrived at the camp, she was nowhere to be found. Eventually she was discovered about a mile away, sketching, her legs dangling above the entrance of the lair of a wild animal.

She sketched. She kept a detailed diary. She wrote poetry and stories. It was she who encouraged me to take up the pen during the evenings, and I wrote essays on many topics for the magazines in Delhi and Calcutta. When the Survey finished, I was made assistant political officer at Ferozepur, which brought me into direct contact with the Sikhs of the Punjab. Together we wrote *The Adventures of an Officer in the Service of Ranjit Singh*, which won considerable acclaim (although not from my superiors, who reckoned I ought not to have used knowledge gained from my political work for writing a novel).

Your mother never flinched from war. News reached us of the horrors and disasters of the Afghan campaign. She feared for my safety, but always encouraged me to advance. It wasn't just a question of my doing my duty. She knew what was in my heart and she willed what I willed. Her brother George was killed in Jagdallak Pass during the appalling retreat. My brother was a prisoner in Kabul. I offered to exchange myself for him. She assented to that decision too, when she heard of it. I fought the better for my country, because my country meant the people that I loved.

Her love in those times of perpetual crisis was an inspiration. I felt myself transformed and indestructible on account of it.

I attribute to her the credit for what I count my boldest exploit. It was just after the first war against the Sikhs. The Treaty of Lahore (largely my own work) obliged them to indemnify us for the cost of our campaign. They were to transfer Kashmir to Golab Singh of Jammu for £1m to raise the money to pay us. I sent Nicholson with him to Kashmir to train his army there. The Kashmiris revolted against the arrangement and drove Golab Singh out. Swift action was called for. I raised an army among the Sikhs and marched to Kashmir. The Sikhs were still smouldering from the defeat of Sobraon. They could have turned on me at any time. I had only my own character to dominate them but that character was inspired by your mother and her trust in the Almighty. Her strength steeled my courage to that task and made me prevail. The rebels gave way.

Many women in those times coped with the anguish of grief through resignation, through silence and prayer. Your mother always found expression for her feelings. In 1843 she lost a child and wrote this poem, which she sent to me for my birthday:

> *Oh how many a hope and fear*
> *Has lived and died within the year*
> *Since, in heart sickening agony*
> *I listened for my infant's cry:*
> *And gave my silent offspring birth*
> *Only to lay it in the earth.*
>
> *God's will be done, but none can tell*
> *No other heart can guess how well,*
> *A mother loves her blighted child*
> *That never stirred and never smiled.*

Your mother's love did not stop at the boundaries of her own family. When I conceived the idea of founding schools for the children of European soldiers born in

India, who would otherwise have been doomed to the miseries of barracks life, she gave the scheme her whole-hearted support. How many women, anxious for the welfare of her own little ones, would so willingly consign a proportion of their income to the care of others? She was willing too, to relinquish entirely the royalties I earned from my writings for this charitable purpose.

She cared deeply for Nicholson, Abbot, Edwardes, Daly and the other young men who ruled the Punjab under my guidance. She warned Nicholson about his anger and intemperate speech, his excessive use of the lash upon the native population. On her death bed she bequeathed her Bible to him. She regretted that he had no wife of his own. She encouraged him to be open to the moral influence of Herbert Edwardes. I think she would have been pleased to learn that Nicholson immediately went to live with Edwardes when ill-health obliged his wife to return to England.

It was always my conviction that Indians as far as possible should be let run their own affairs. We should be their partners or guides, where appropriate. They trust not to systems, but personalities. For the Sikhs, I was the Empire. By the Treaty of Lahore they invited me to administer the country until the young Regent could do it himself. I was placed by them in the position of trustee of the whole country. I delegated my authority to Nicholson, Abbot, Edwardes and the others, each man taking nearly complete responsibility for the region of which he had charge. Since each individual was encouraged to take decisions on the spot, little was referred to the Governor-General's staff. The transformation of the country within a year was remarkable.

I underestimated the degree of resentment and suspicion my method aroused in government circles, encouraged as I was by Hardinge himself. There were murmurs that mine was too Irish a way of doing things, I was undermining the government. The fact that I had not been afforded the resources to act in any other way was apparently of no consequence.

When Hardinge retired from office, I accepted his invitation to take my furlough then and accompany him on his journey home.

Dalhousie was 'warned' about me when he arrived. When the revolt occurred at Multan, he could have acted swiftly to put it down. Instead, he let the thing fester and grow. I returned as soon as possible. I could have made terms. But the whole atmosphere had changed. I encountered a governor-general whose declared task was 'the utter destruction and prostration of the Sikh power'. I found myself at Chillianwallah, with Nicholson, trying to inject some system into Gough's manic strategy. At Gujerat the Sikh leaders sued for terms – but I was instructed to reply that nothing less than their total and unconditional surrender would be accepted. They were too proud for that.

Everyone wanted to blame McNaughten, the Resident at Kabul, for the disaster in Afghanistan. In defending him, I pointed out that that real problem was the inadequacies of our military system. Only dissension among our enemies had turned our position in India from that of commercial factors to lords over emperors. That plus our own courage and discipline. The ease with which our conquests had been accomplished made us neglect the standard rules of military occupation. We ruled by the sword, but everywhere our military means were insufficient. I said that the same causes operated for our first successes in both India and Afghanistan. I said that the mistakes by which we had lost Afghanistan might one day cause us to lose India as well.

The failings of our military system now stand exposed throughout India. We must fight or perish.

I have a wonderful horse called Ludakee. Do you remember him? He has served me well. If anything happens to me, I will give him to your cousin, who fights bravely beside me here every day. You will not mind that, will you?

Pray for me as I do for you.

Henry Lawrence

SEVEN

Corunna, Spain, January 1809

THE SITUATION WAS GRIM. British resistance having collapsed under an onslaught directed by Napoleon, Sir John Moore conducted a rear-guard action to evacuate the troops from the port of Corunna. Fighting concentrated on the suburb of Elvina. Hardinge was instructed to call up two battalions of Guards to replace the 42nd and 50th divisions, whose advance had faltered. When the reserves moved into position, Hardinge returned to Sir John to report.

A shot from a French battery knocked Moore out of the saddle. His left shoulder was shattered. Only a piece of skin connected it to his arm. The ribs over his heart were smashed and the flesh was blown away from them. The muscles of his chest were in shreds. Hardinge used his sash in a vain attempt to stem the flow of blood from the enormous wound. Then, when six men eased the

General into a blanket to carry him out of the firing line, Hardinge used the sash to support the upper body. But the hilt of Sir John's sword entered the wound – Hardinge began to unbuckle the belt.

'It is as well as it is, I should rather it go out of the field with me.'

Hardinge would never forget those words.

Moore died, fearing that blame for the reversals would fall on him. But the army escaped. So, had young Hardinge attended the death of a hero or a failure? In April 1817 an obscure Irish newspaper, the *Newry Telegraph*, published some anonymous verses which determined the issue.

> *Not a drum was heard, not a funeral note*
> *As his corse to the rampart we hurried;*
> *Not a soldier discharged his farewell shot*
> *O'er the grave where our hero was buried.*
>
> *We buried him darkly at dead of night,*
> *The sods with our bayonets turning,*
> *By the struggling moonbeams' misty light*
> *And the lantern dimly burning ...*
>
> *Lightly they'll talk of the spirit that's gone*
> *And o'er his cold ashes upbraid him –*
> *But little he'll reck, if they let him sleep on*
> *In the grave where a Briton has laid him ...*
>
> *Slowly and sadly we laid him down,*
> *From the field of his fame fresh and gory;*
> *We carved not a line and we raised not a stone,*
> *But we left him alone in his glory.*

'The Death of Sir John Moore' was an instant success which secured the immortality of its subject. Byron, regretfully disclaiming it, pronounced it 'the most perfect ode in the language'. The revelation that the author was an obscure clergyman from County Kildare, the Reverend Charles Wolfe, prompted the raising of unfriendly comments. How could the moon have lit up a ceremony which took place at 8 a.m.? Lanterns would not have been necessary. Moreover, the ground had been disturbed for the burial of another officer two to four hours previously.

Hardinge noted that the exposure of these absurdities undermined the poem's popularity not one jot. Wherever he went, people he had never met asked him about the last moments of Sir John Moore – he was bathed in reflected glory. He wondered whether his reputation might not have shone more brightly in its own light had a poet taken up the theme of the battle of Albuera.

What happened was this. It's May 1811 and, once again, a grim situation: half the allied force has been wiped out by the battalions of Maréchal Soult. The British commander dithers, contemplates a retreat. Hardinge seizes the initiative: he gallops up to Sir Galbraith Lowry Cole and tells him that absolutely everything depends upon his sending his fusiliers forward, now. Cole advances immediately and forces Soult to retire.

It should have been enough to make Hardinge a hero.

The quarter-master-general, in his account of the battle, gave Hardinge credit for the decisive action. Henry brought this report to the attention of George Napier who, in his *History of the War in the Peninsula*, wrote that 'Hardinge, on his own responsibility, boldly ordered Cole's advance.' But Cole disputed this. He claimed that he had made up his own mind to charge before Hardinge approached him. This put Hardinge in a spot. He could understand Cole's being peeved, but he could scarcely pass over the reflection upon himself notwithstanding. He insisted the charge was due to the 'urgent pressure' he had placed upon Cole. Napier was in a spot too. He could scarcely ignore the statement of the man who had actually led the charge. In a subsequent edition he wrote that Hardinge had 'strongly urged' the action, but dropped the suggestion that he had ordered it.

What were people to think? Was Hardinge the hero of the battle of Albuera? Was he a glory-hunter inflating his own reputation at the expense of others? No verses on the matter ever appeared.

Arthur Wellesley, the well-known warrior from County Meath, had no doubts about the affair. Hardinge was made of the right stuff. He appointed him military and diplomatic representative to the staff of Blucher, the Prussian commander, for the Waterloo campaign. It proved a role of crucial importance since Blucher's last-minute intervention determined the outcome of the battle.

A day of onsets and despair!
Dash'd on every rocky square
Their surging charges foam'd themselves away
Last, the Prussian trumpet blew;
Thro' the long-tormented air
Heaven flash'd a sudden jubilant ray,
And down we swept and charged and overthrew
So great a soldier taught us there,

What long enduring hearts could do
In that world's-earthquake, Waterloo!

The chief difficulty Hardinge coped with was Blucher's madness. He believed that he was pregnant, with an elephant, fathered upon him by a French soldier. 'Je me sens elephant, là!' he would say, pointing to his stomach.

Hardinge also had to cope with the fact that his left hand was shot at Ligny and had to be amputated. In recognition of his outstanding service, Wellesley presented him with no less a prize than Napoleon's sword. In addition, he drew Hardinge into the inner circle of the caste which dominated his country and much of the world.

He married a wonderful woman from County Donegal. She had large oval eyes, brown hair and a pale skin which suggested that her constitution was not the strongest. Whatever she may have lacked in terms of physical strength, Emily Jane Stewart more than compensated in terms of lineage and position. She was a daughter of the Marquess of Londonderry, a half-sister of Viscount Castlereagh. Noting that his brother-in-law's quite phenomenal unpopularity was in part attributable to his responsibility for the so-called 'Peterloo' massacre –

I met with murder on the way
It had the name of Castlereagh

– one of Hardinge's reforms as Secretary for War was to prohibit the military's firing upon mobs.

His career advanced steadily. Beginning with an appointment as Clerk of Ordnance, it included two stints as Secretary for War and two as Irish Secretary. This occasioned his taking up residence in the Phoenix Park where, at many soirées hosted in true Londonderry style by Emily Jane, he renewed acquaintance with his old Peninsular brother-in-arms, Hugh Gough. A high point of this period was the introduction of legislation which sorted out the thorny issue of tithes, more or less. Hardinge was under no illusion about the impact of any kind of legislation in quelling Irish disturbances. He argued that, 'from the temper of the people', a sufficient force should always be distributed throughout the country. Since the menace was constant, the remedy should be constant too.

In 1844 Hardinge went to India to replace his wife's brother-in-law, Lord Ellenborough, as Governor-General. En route he crossed Egypt, ostensibly out of curiosity, but secretly to make a military report on the defences of Aden. He saw Cairo, the pyramids, the Nile and other wonders of that land which Ellenborough had long dreamed of occupying with British troops, himself and Hardinge at their head.

But the dream, at least so far as the husbands of the Londonderrys were concerned, was not to be.

And the dream of India was not to be for Emily Jane. She was on the point of embarking at Nice when she suddenly took ill. She was obliged to remain in Europe.

An unprecedented era of reform marked the first months of Hardinge's administration. He reduced the Salt Tax. He started the Grand Trunk Railway Line, which he foresaw would bring huge benefits in the military, political and commercial spheres. He banned Sunday labour. He suppressed the horrible custom of the Kandhi people of offering human victims to the Earth-God. Seeing the advantages to both the governors and the governed of the spread of education, he issued a proclamation which held out the prospect of a career in the civil service to Hindu and Muslim youths who distinguished themselves at school. This action met with a very positive response from many native gentlemen.

So it came about that, in March of 1845, Hardinge found himself distributing prizes at Muslim and Hindu schools, marvelling at the excellent standard of the delivery of Shakespearean verse on the part of the pupils:

> *O, pardon me, thou bleeding piece of earth*
> *That I am meek and gentle with these butchers!*
> *Thou art the ruins of the noblest man*
> *That ever lived in the tide of time*
> *Woe to the hands that shed this costly blood!*

It wasn't a case of these speeches being trotted out in parrot-like fashion. Hardinge expressed his pleasure at 'the intelligence and fluency' with which pupils explained to him the verse they recited. Thunderous applause greeted his announcement of the appointment of one boy to the position of deputy magistrate on account of his proficiency in the English language.

He did not neglect military matters. Alerted by Ellenborough to sinister developments in the kingdom of the Sikhs following the death of their great leader, Runjit Singh, he quietly moved troops and artillery to various stations along the frontier. When at last the Sikhs poured into British territory, Hardinge was ready for them.

He immediately offered his services, as second-in-command, to Hugh Gough. Some, in the light of future developments, criticized him for this diminution of his

53

responsibility as Governor-General. Others, like Herbert Edwardes, approved it: 'We are among those who think that to lead on a wing of a British Army against the enemies of this country can derogate from the dignity of no man.' The middle view was that this decision of Hardinge's was simply to show the respect and courtesy one officer and gentleman owed another.

At Muckee, the Khalsa – the ancient warrior/religious caste which formed the Sikh army – impressed even veterans of the Peninsula with the ferocity of their artillery fire, their tenacity and cohesion, despite being forced from the field. Hardinge approached the next encounter, at Ferozeshah, with foreboding. Low trees and undergrowth separated the British from the Sikhs, whose trenches and batteries had been established with great skill.

Hardinge was sharing some refreshments with his entourage when Gough rode up to him.

'Sir Henry, if we attack at once I promise you a splendid victory,' said Gough.

Hardinge blanched. The plan had been to wait until Littler arrived. He signalled to Gough to accompany him to a grove of trees some yards away where they would be out of earshot of their subordinates. What passed between them there was not divulged by Hardinge until many years later. It seems that Gough kept insisting that now was the time to attack. Sir Henry eventually threatened to use his civil power to forbid any advance until after Littler arrived. Sir Hugh had no option but to desist.

Littler did not arrive until 1 p.m. It took until 3 p.m. for the line to be drawn up. Now only three hours of daylight remained. Was that sufficient? Hardinge felt there was no alternative but to attack. They were far from a source of water. Tej Singh was on his way with reinforcements.

Gough gave the order to advance.

The fire from the Sikh batteries was tremendous. The Sepoys proved as plucky as the Portuguese Hardinge had led in the Peninsula, but it was the 'brave British infantry' which carried the guns. If some lads who had never heard a bullet before fled when they reached the guns, what of it? They had done their duty.

Darkness fell when the advance reached the Sikh camp. Tents and forage caught fire. Live shells were exploding, and loose powder. All was chaos. The troops had to stop in their tracks, lie down and wait until morning. It was a desperate position, for the Sikhs were expert at night-time manoeuvres. Many officers begged the commanders to withdraw. But Gough and Hardinge were adamant that they must remain where they were.

Gough went round his men saying, 'Hold your fire to the last! Trust to your bayonets!'

Sir Henry sent Napoleon's sword to a safe place, a precaution which did not escape the attention of Sir Hugh.

Day dawned. Thanks to the intervention of the man in pyjamas, both armies quit the scene.

In London, the government became alarmed. The Sikhs were still fighting, despite two engagements with the largest British force ever put into the field on the sub-continent. Gough was presumed to be at fault. Instructions were forwarded to Sir Henry to the effect that he must take command himself, but the letter containing them did not arrive until after the next battle.

The enemy massed at Sobraon. The British bided their time, waiting for a supply train to arrive. The fear was that the Khalsa might divide their forces and fall back upon the strongholds of Lahore, Govindgarh and Amritsar. At that time of year, given the balance of resources which would then be available to both sides, the British could scarcely hope to prevail, Hardinge well knew.

Every morning he led a good-humoured party out for a gallop to reconnoitre the Sikh positions. He rode Miani, his favourite Arab charger. They would watch General Gilbert, who was a celebrated pig-sticker, hunt boars through the jungle, without interference from the enemy.

Once the supply-train arrived, only one outcome was possible. The British guns pounded the Sikh batteries, which only fell however to the bayonet. The enemy showed impressive discipline in retiring in good order to the bridge across which they planned to escape. But quickly they were hemmed in by the infantry. Then the bridge collapsed under the weight of horses, guns, men and carriages. The water was thronged with desperate figures straining for the shore. Sir Hugh ordered the artillery up to the river bank. Volley after volley was loosed upon the mass of confused, half-drowning men, none of whom surrendered.

The Sutlej ran red with the blood of the Khalsa.

Some people objected that this was churlish treatment to mete out to so noble a foe. Others were conscious of the heinous mutilations the Sikhs had served upon the wounded and dying during the night-time hours at Ferozeshah, acts they had vowed to avenge. The middle view was that it was necessary to fire upon the horde in the river, because had the Sikhs not been utterly destroyed, they would have rallied again.

The lowest estimate reckoned the Sikh dead at

Sobraon at 8000. British losses were 320 killed and 2000 wounded for that battle. The review of the army of the Sutlej, when at last it was held some weeks later, proved a moving affair for Hardinge and Gough. The numbers of their beloved Peninsular regiments, whose veterans had borne the brunt of the campaign, were halved.

But after Sobraon it was on to the enchanted city of Lahore, with its mosques and minarets, bazaars and palaces, its winding alleyways and scented gardens. Hardinge was determined to diminish Sikh strength, punish them in the eyes of Asia. He had not the resources to make a success of annexation – but a British Resident with considerable powers would be installed at Lahore. He demanded their famous diamond, the Koh-I-Noor, as a gift for Queen Victoria. They had to transfer to the Company a fertile district between the river Beas and the Sutlej, whose revenue was worth £500,000, and Kashmir was to be transferred to Golab Singh, who had declined the invitation to take up arms.

Hardinge's son Charles, like his father a keen amateur painter, took the opportunity to make a sketch of Lal Singh, notorious lover of the equally notorious Rani or Queen Regent. He was the most strikingly handsome man Hardinge had ever seen. But it was Lal Singh who, in breach of the terms of the Treaty, enticed Shaikh-Imam-ud-In of Kashmir to revolt, thereby necessitating an amendment to the treaty. A British minister would carry on the government of the Punjab during the minority of the Raja, Dhulip Singh.

Two hundred fifty-six Sikh guns were hauled in triumph across India by the victorious army, deeply impressing the natives.

Hardinge was raised to the peerage and voted an annuity of £3000 by parliament for his efforts. The East India Company awarded him a further £5000, but Emily Jane declined this on his behalf. Whatever difficulties there had been with Hugh Gough under the stresses and strains of the honours awarded the commander-in-chief, Hardinge paid him the highest tribute he could conceive of: 'I am most gratified that my excellent and distinguished friend has received the honours he so nobly won. He is a fine specimen of an English officer and English gentleman.'

During the short time left to him in India, Hardinge renewed his outstanding programme of reform. Against all opposition he sustained the Ganges Canal scheme of irrigation, which was to prove so successful in averting famine and making the country profitable. He endeavoured to stamp out the barbarous customs of suttee – whereby widows hurled themselves or were hurled upon the funeral pyres of their husbands – and infanticide (the eight-year-old Dhulip Singh had shocked his British protectors with his accounts of baby sisters being put in sacks and flung into the river). He encouraged the cultivation of tea and the preservation of ancient monuments. A great admirer of the Taj Mahal, he ordered parts of it to be repaired, as well as the palace of Agra. He arranged for records to be made of all these buildings by means of the novel art of photography.

Not all native art met with his approval, however. He drew the line at the ornament placed on top of the Kutab Minar at Delhi, an item his son Charles later described as 'unseemly and grotesque'. Hardinge ordered this piece of sculpture to be removed. (Apparently it depicted a Hindu

God of outsize proportions engaging in the act of sexual intercourse from a standing position.)

He maintained the strength of European troops and reduced that of the Sepoys, whose numbers were an unnecessary burden upon the exchequer now that the war was over. To warn its Prince of the consequences of continued misrule, he visited the independent state of Oudh. There he attended an unusual tiger-hunt, unusual in that some seventy elephants were employed to beat out the jungle and raise the tigers. Despite his handicap, Hardinge was an excellent shot – he used to rest the barrel of his rifle upon the remains of his left hand.

On the eve of his departure, European and native residents of the Presidency of Calcutta congratulated Hardinge in the warmest terms. They valued 'his pacific sentiment' but also the 'imperishable honour won by British arms on the banks of the Sutlej' when he had been forced to take the field. They declared their intention to preserve in Calcutta 'some personal memorial of one who has received the highest honour from the Sovereign and the thanks of his countrymen while ruling this vast empire'.

And so it was back to England with Henry Lawrence, a tiger and Himalayan pheasants for the Queen, some Chinese dogs, and not least his beloved Miani from whom he could not bring himself to part. As on the way out, he travelled through Egypt for the purpose of gathering military intelligence, having been asked to report on the route between Kossur, on the Red Sea and the Nile – the route which was indeed used during the eventual occupation.

It was 1848, the year of revolutions. He had to circumvent Paris on account of the fall of the Orleans dynasty. He was no sooner home than sent to Ireland on a special mission to deal with the Smith O'Brien riots there. But in the event the outbreak was crushed before his services were actively engaged.

The Duke of Wellington re-appointed him to his old job as Clerk of the Ordnance. Then the Duke himself passed away.

Lead out the pageant, sad and slow
As fits an universal woe,
Let the long procession go
And let the sorrowing crowd about it grow
And let the mournful martial music blow
The last great Englishman is low.

O good grey head which all men knew,
O voice from which their omens all men drew,
O iron nerve to true occasion true,
O fall'n at length that tower of strength
Which stood four-square to all the winds that blew!
Such was he whom we deplore.
The long self-sacrifice of life is o'er.
The great World-victor's will be seen no more.

Hardinge was appointed to step into the Duke's shoes as head of the army. He purchased 9000 acres at Aldershot to provide a much-needed training-ground. He replaced that old favourite weapon of the infantryman, Brown Bess, with the rifle. He established the school of musketry at Hythe … all seemed set fair for a fitting end to an excellent career.

Then came the Crimean War.

As one mind-numbing account succeeded another of

the incompetence, stupidity and brutal indifference to the fate of their own men on the part of the caste-representatives who ruled the army, the glories of India, the Punjab, Waterloo and the Peninsula seemed reduced to ashes. Hardinge had to accept responsibility. It was the Duke's system which he had inherited, but the Duke was beyond criticism. The stupidest action of all was removed to the realm of the imagination by a poem.

> *Theirs not to reason why*
> *Theirs but to do or die,*
> *Into the valley of death*
> *Rode the six hundred.*

But no one wrote a poem for Lord Hardinge. Instead it fell to his lot to hand a report on the conduct of the war to his sovereign at Aldershot. This was too much for him to bear. He was struck down by paralysis in the act of doing so.

The end came soon afterwards, in September 1856. There was no pomp about the funeral – his own labourers carried Hardinge from Penshurst to the beautiful churchyard at Ferdcambe, where Ellenborough and Gough stood by the coffin on which were laid a head-dress and the sword of Napoleon.

EIGHT

FOLEY MADE two statues of Earl Canning. One stands in the north-west transept of Westminster Abbey, between two other famous Cannings. His father George is on his right-hand side, his father's cousin Stratford is on his left. Stratford, the legendary ambassador to the Turks, looks crafty. George, the legendary foreign minister, looks somewhat dashing.

A large cloak is draped around the Earl's shoulders. His arms are folded. His eyes – set between a noble brow and an aquiline nose – gaze steadily into the distance. The shape of the stone wonderfully embodies the qualities that distinguished this Canning in the minds of his contemporaries: imperturbability, stoicism, reflection, calm, wisdom. His impassive countenance contrasts with the animated features of his kinsmen.

He might have been represented differently, in other

company. With his grandfather George, for example, who came to London from Garvagh when he was disinherited on account of an attachment 'of which the family disapproved', which probably means he became involved with a Catholic. He was called to the bar, wrote for the newspapers and published a book of poetry. He fell in love with one Mary Anne Costello, 'beautiful and penniless', a Catholic from County Mayo. They say that he died of a broken heart when he found that he could not support his wife and children. Earl Canning wrote poetry too. At Oxford, he won a prize for a Latin composition upon the theme of the captivity of Caratacus. And he too died of a broken heart. At the age of twenty-three he married Charlotte Stuart, the eldest daughter of Lord Stuart de Rothsay. When she succumbed to jungle fever in 1861, Canning plunged into a profound grief. He died the following year.

At Eton he was remembered for 'intelligence, accuracy and painstakingness' rather than for refined scholarship or any remarkable powers of composition. At Oxford he took a first in Classics. He was the friend and contemporary of Dalhousie and Ellenborough, who invited him to India as his private secretary. Canning declined this offer. He became instead Under-Secretary to Lord Aberdeen at the Foreign Office. When Sir Robert Peel's ministry fell he rejected an offer to become Foreign Secretary, as he felt that he could not give the new administration his complete support. After some years in opposition, he came back into the cabinet as Post-Master General.

His industry was unremitting, and his name became a byword for prudence. He made decisions only after a scrupulous enquiry into all the facts. Some people said that he was too cautious, that he enquired into too many facts before doing anything at all.

Canning pooh-poohed such criticism.

He surprised the carpers by introducing an innovation which, even at the time, was estimated to have far-reaching significance: the practice of submitting an annual report to Parliament. The affairs of the Post Office were subject to public scrutiny for the first time. This made for an improved service.

He made such a favourable impression overall that he was invited to succeed Dalhousie as Governor-General of India. Some people wondered (aloud) whether he was really up to the job. Apart from having a famous name, was there anything to him? At the traditional farewell dinner hosted by the East India Company, he made a strong impact upon the distinguished guests. His 'noble Canning brow' was compared to a 'block of white marble'. He spoke of the wonder of India, a situation unexampled in human history, where 150 million people submitted in 'peace and contentment' to the government of a few thousand strangers and aliens.

Through his annexation of the Punjab, Pegaa, Nagpur, Satara, Jansi and Oudh, Dalhousie had added some £4m to the annual revenues of British India. Canning quickly found himself in need of the extra money. He had to fit out Sir James Outram's expedition to Afghanistan to drive the Persians from Herat. In one way he could compare this to the type of thing he had done at the Post Office. Both operations were about determining the most efficient way of moving objects from one point on the map to another. Paying out the government's money to Sir James Outram for the purpose was one thing, however, paying it out to Dost Mohammed, the Emir of Kabul, to enable him to march on Herat was quite another. This was the policy advocated by Herbert Edwardes. Canning decided to hold an enquiry.

He learned that John Nicholson, for one, was against it. What was the point of an alliance with the most treacherous people on the face of the earth, a race utterly false and faithless, even among themselves? Nicholson frankly declared that he could not so much as bring himself to meet the Afghans. He would be tempted to shoot one. The enquiry soon fizzled out, when Outram made short work of the Persians.

The next problem for Canning was the Sepoy Mutiny of 1857.

There were a number of factors involved. New terms of service in the army led Brahmans to fear that they might be forced to travel overseas despite their religion's prohibition on doing so. Dalhousie's policy of annexation was coupled with some efforts at proselytizing, which grounded a widespread fear among the 150 million that the British meant to take, not just their land and money, but their religion also. This fear concentrated on the question of cartridges. It was believed that cartridges had been issued which were greased with the fat of the cow (sacred to the Hindu) and the fat of the pig (anathema to the Muslim).

Canning understood the sincerity at least of the Sepoys' objections. And it turned out later that their cartridges had indeed been greased with the abhorrent fat. But their attitude posed a military crisis. What was to be done with troops who refused to handle the cartridges – who refused to obey orders?

Canning counselled a policy of leniency. At first, regiments who rejected the cartridges were disbanded and that only after a careful consideration of the circumstances involved in the particular case. Hardliners in the army criticized Canning for this, and gave him the nickname 'Clemency' Canning. They claimed his softness was encouraging rather than stemming the crisis. If all that insubordinate troops had to fear by the way of punishment was disbandment, they would go right ahead and rebel. Harsher measures were required.

In April of 1857 some ninety of the 3rd Light Cavalry stationed at Meerut refused to receive the cartridges. All were summarily dismissed. Then General Anson, the Commander-in-Chief of the army, ordered that all of them were to be tried by court martial. The sentences were announced to a parade of the whole of the native troops. Each was sentenced to ten years imprisonment with hard labour, a harsh penalty in any climate, but in India one which was tantamount to a lingering death. All the prisoners were then branded with an iron in front of the brigade. The next evening their comrades broke open the jail and set the prisoners free. They shot every European they chanced upon and marched off to Delhi.

The situation in Delhi was never so grim. Everywhere were scenes of carnage, plunder, destruction. Some officers and soldiers, the remnant of the garrison, fled the city before the onslaught of the mutineers, dragging the surviving members of their families with them, but leaving behind some fifty or so women and children of the commercial class. These wretches had no opportunity to escape. All they could do was band together and barricade themselves into a strong house in their district. But the mutineers broke down their barricade and carried them all off to the Palace of the King of Delhi, the native monarch resurgent on the tide of anarchy, and thrust these defenceless Christians into an underground dungeon. They had little light, air or food, but much abuse. One of the English ladies was asked how the natives would be treated if the English became powerful again. 'Just as you have treated our husbands and children,' she replied.

Next day the captives were told that they were being taken to a better place. By now some few men were among them. A rope encircled them, as if they were animals. They were herded into a courtyard where a great crowd had gathered, shouting and screaming abuse at the Feringhee. Who could describe the terror felt by that little band, huddled together in the midst of that savage throng? Gunfire opened up upon them, and their terror ceded to blind panic and despair. For a moment it seemed there might be some respite – a bullet struck an attendant of the King and the guns fell silent. But the hope was short-lived. The soldiers waded into the Christians with sword, bayonet and dagger, butchering them all. Only Mrs Aldwell escaped, with her three children, by pretending to be a Muslim.

The bodies were piled upon carts and taken to the Jumna river, where they were dumped.

At Cawnpore in June, things were even worse. Worn out by hunger and thirst, encumbered by the presence of many sick and wounded, women and children, in their ranks, the garrison surrendered to the troops commanded by Nana Sahib. He, through the agency of an English lady whose identity, perhaps mercifully, has never been positively ascertained – some people say it was Mrs

Greenaway – promised safe passage to Allahabad to all subjects of Her Most Gracious Majesty Queen Victoria who were willing to lay down their arms and who were unconnected with the acts of Lord Dalhousie.

And so it was agreed. The British would give up their position, their guns and their money. Each should march out bearing his arms and sixty rounds of ammunition. Nana Sahib was to provide carriages to bring the women, children and the wounded to the river. There a flotilla of boats, with a supply of food for the journey, was to be ready.

Early next day the survivors of the siege walked or were carried to the river, battered and bedraggled, worn out and starving. They were due to embark close by a village named the Suttee Chaura Chaut, where there were English residences and the Hindu temple of the monkey (Hindeo). Many Sepoys crowded around their former officers, engaging them in conversation, remarking upon their miserable condition, offering words of advice and encouragement. Old Colonel Ewart, who on account of his wounds was being carried on a palanquin, fell behind the main party. His wife walked beside him. Soon they were surrounded by soldiers of his regiment, who jeered and insulted the aged couple.

'Isn't this a fine parade, Colonel? Isn't the regiment looking well?'

Then the Sepoys hacked Ewart and his wife to pieces.

By nine o'clock all the others were aboard the flimsy riverboats, which had thatched roofs. Because it was the dry season in India the river was low. The boats were moored in the shallows. The banks of the river were thronged with people from the town and surrounding countryside who had come to watch the departure. The hour of deliverance seemed to be at hand. But it was not to be. A trumpet sounded. The native boatmen leaped from the vessels and swam ashore. The Sepoys opened up a murderous fire from the banks. Cinders were flung upon the roofs of the boats which instantly burst into flame. Men struggled desperately to steer the boats out into the channels but most would not budge and were swallowed in the general inferno. The sick and wounded from these boats suffocated or were burnt. Others, including women and children, trusted to the water where they were shot down or put to the sword by the mounted soldiers who pursued them. Those who recovered the shore were bayoneted or taken prisoner. At last Nana Sahib ordered that no more English women and children were to be killed, though all the men were to be slain. One boat alone, manned by officers and men, drifted from the scene. Four survived two days of savage fighting to tell the story.

The captives at Delhi counted some four men in their number. All were held for weeks in a house known as the Beebeeghur (the babies' place). At length, as the army of deliverance approached, Nana Sahib ordered these men to be brought out and killed in his presence. Then he ordered a general slaughter: the Sepoys were to shoot through the doors and windows of the house at the women and children. The Sepoys, however, had no stomach for the task and aimed their rifles instead at the walls and ceilings of the place. Nana Sahib threatened to blow these men from guns. He summoned six butchers from the bazaar, three Muslims and three Hindus. These six moved through the house as though it were a shambles, stabbing the hearts and cutting the throats of the inhabitants.

Not all were killed. Witnesses noted that, during the night, while the shrieking ceased, the groaning did not. Next day, some little children emerged unscathed from beneath the heaps of mangled carcasses. The living and the dead were all flung indiscriminately down a well – two hundred women and children.

At Jhansi, in June, the situation was similar to that at Delhi and Cawnpore. The pressure upon the garrison grew more intense with each passing day. Messengers were sent to the Ranee, begging her to grant safe passage from the fort. All were murdered. The Ranee, still smarting from her humiliation at the hands of Dalhousie, sent more weapons to the besiegers. Treachery within was discovered just before the gates were opened. But then Captain Gordon, the inspiration of the defenders, was struck in the face by a sniper's bullet as, perhaps foolishly, he looked through a window. His death put everyone into a great depression. Next day they put up the flag for a truce. The besiegers solemnly swore that none would be harmed if they laid down their arms and surrendered the fort. The defenders had no choice but to agree. They left the fort in sad procession. Immediately, all were set upon and tied with ropes. They were brought to a place near a clump of trees. The women and children were separated from the men. All sixty were put to the sword. For three days their bodies were exposed. Then all were tossed into two shallow pits.

Stories of such atrocities were brought to Calcutta by refugees from British communities all over the North-West provinces. Horror mounted upon horror with endless accounts of torture, rape and mutilation. Every outrage one could imagine came to be charged, not merely against the mutinous Sepoys, but against the black races as a whole.

From among the British population there arose a great clamour for retribution against the perpetrators of these heinous deeds. Many were convinced that straightforward hanging was not enough. Since there were different degrees of punishment for theft, the argument ran, why not for murder? The view was well expressed in a letter John Nicholson wrote to Herbert Edwardes, seeking his support for a Bill which would authorize more cruel forms of execution:

> *Let us propose a Bill for the flaying alive, impalement or burning of the murderers of the women and children at Delhi. The idea of simply hanging the perpetrators of such atrocities is maddening. I wish that I were in that part of the world, that if necessary I might take the law into my own hands.*

Nicholson based his argument firmly upon the Bible, where it is laid down that stripes shall be meted out according to faults.

> *If I had them in my power today, and knew that I were to die tomorrow, I would inflict the most excruciating tortures I could think of on them with a perfectly easy conscience.*

It was a time when the most pious Christians in India warned against the dangers of compassion. General Neill advised Henry Tucker, the Commissioner for Benares, that natural tenderness had to be crucified as much as lust:

The Word of God gives no authority to the modern tenderness for human life which would save even the murderer. It is necessary in all eastern lands to establish a fear and awe of the government. We must be sternly, rigorously just against all treason, violence and treachery, and hand down a tradition of our severity.

These were the conditions in which Canning sought to maintain the authority of his government. At first, he strove to prevent the mutiny from becoming an outright race war. For weeks he resisted pressure to dismiss his own personal bodyguard of native troops. When, seeing the disarming of native regiments throughout the country and the heightening anger of the Europeans, the native population of Calcutta bought arms, Canning extended the order for disarming them to the European population as well. Likewise, he extended his censorship of the native press to the European press in a series of measures dubbed the 'Gagging Acts'. This earned him the enmity of large sections of his own people, who called for his removal from office.

In May and June the Legislative Council passed a series of Acts for the trial of offences relating to the army and offences against the state. These established Martial Law. Tribunals manned by officers could pass the death sentence for a wide range of crimes. Even these measures did not silence Canning's critics. 'Insufficient. Too late,' they gibed, in a time-honoured phrase of the post-office. Now Canning strove to control the judicial forces he had unleashed:

The use of the utmost severity in law is necessary to strike terror into the minds of the evilly disposed among the people. Once this is done punishment should be meted out with discrimination. Otherwise people will be driven to desperation.

For this he was accused of 'indiscriminate forgiveness'. Lenity towards any element within the conspiracy was reckoned to

excite contempt and invite attack. It shows the government of India so powerless that it allows the blood of English and Christian subjects of Her Majesty to flow in torrents, and their wives, sisters and daughters to be outraged and dishonoured without adequate retribution.

In the event, retribution proved more than adequate.

Whole villages were burnt, along with their entire populations. Canning's argument that such actions might cause famine and exasperate the innocent along with the guilty went unheeded. He reported to Parliament that 'the aged, women and children, are sacrificed, along with those guilty of rebellion'.

When General Neill retook Cawnpore, those held to be responsible for the massacre were whipped and forced to clean the blood from the Beebee-gurh, often with their tongues, before being hanged. Throughout the country, Sepoys whose regiments had no part in the rebellion, or who had been absent from regiments that did revolt, were hunted down and shot by bands of armed civilians.

Around Allahabad, for three months, the soldiers hanged virtually everyone they could lay hands on. The trials were a farce. Branches of trees, signposts, crossbeams – all were festooned with dangling black corpses. Twenty blacks compensated for one white life. The town was full of the stench of death. All day and every day the

74

death-carts plied their loads to the Ganges whose waters carried away no fewer than six thousand victims.

Many, soldiers and civilians, saw an opportunity for sport. They went out a-hunting blacks as they would game. 'Pea-fowl partridges and Pandies rose together, but the latter gave the best sport. Lancers ran a tilt at a wretch who had taken to the open for his covert.' Englishmen acknowledged that 'peppering away at niggers' was altogether great fun. Still others saw an opportunity for profit, and extorted money from wealthy natives who were forced to give up their fortunes to save their lives.

While his unpopularity prevented him from being given credit until much later, Canning made a number of decisions which were crucial to the suppression of the revolt. By giving Henry Lawrence military command at Lucknow at an early stage, he enabled him to take the steps which provided for the garrison's survival in that city. He established the retaking of Delhi as the military priority. He overruled John Lawrence's proposal to abandon territory beyond the Indus should certain extreme circumstances arise.

Afterwards, the government decided that India required a change of management and transferred responsibility from the East India Company to the Crown. Canning became the first viceroy. He settled down to the administrative work for which he had been sent to India in the first place. He reorganized the army. He took steps to restore the confidence of native chiefs in British rule. He gave his support to a scheme for the education of the children of Eurasians and poor Europeans. Believing that the government of India needed extra money, he determined to introduce income tax. For this he incurred vilification from the English on a scale which surpassed what he had experienced in the blackest days of the mutiny. It left him unmoved.

Charlotte's death proved a crisis of a different order because his own feelings went into revolt. He had no language with which to express or order them. He was overwhelmed.

NINE

FTER WE HAD CLEANED out one bank, Francisco and Dermot and myself crossed the street and entered another one. We got eight thousand in the first, twelve in the second. Then we all jumped into the car and drove off.

A lorry pulled across the street to block our escape.

'Jesus!' said Babington.

'Fuck him!' said Francisco.

I didn't say anything because I saw immediately what to do – drive up on the footpath. There was buckets of room and I just went ahead and did it. But the others felt we were faced with a crisis. If you don't have a driving sense, you can't judge a situation like that. Babington freaked out for a few moments, which was how he came to give me a wrong direction as we left the town. The turns we should have been making just weren't coming up.

It took us three miles before we finally identified the mistake we'd made. And we couldn't turn around and go back to Carlow to get on the right road. The trouble was, beyond the fact that we were somewhere in the region of south Carlow and Kilkenny, we didn't know where we were.

We had to get off that road. I chose a track going through a forest. It turned out to lead only to a gate to a farm.

'Decisions! More decisions!' I said.

A few acres of forestry covered the hills around us. We decided to bury the stuff there and then and to hide the car as best we could. We made separate piles of guns, clothes and money. Just as we were beginning to feel a little secure, I saw a man staring at us from the brow of a hill a hundred yards beyond the gate. When he saw me looking at him, he turned on his heel and disappeared down the far side of the hill. I could just make out the roof of a house some distance beyond it. The track we were on went in that direction on the far side of the gate.

'Back in the car! We're going to have to grab this guy!' I said.

So we opened the gate, got back in the car and followed the track around the hill, putting on our balaclavas and so forth as we went. I realized that neither Stephen nor Babington was challenging my suggestion.

We soon found ourselves driving alongside the man who had spotted us. He was shouting instructions to a sheepdog some fields away.

'Go on, King!'

It was weird listening to him. I reckoned it was his way of coping with fear. It was as though he were crying to the dog for help which the dog couldn't give him. He put off the moment of actually looking at us for as long as he could.

'Hello,' I said.

He didn't say anything.

'Is that your house? Is that where you're going?'

He nodded. 'We need help. We're coming home with you for a little chat.' He nodded again and kept on walking.

'We're revolutionaries,' I said. 'We're honourable people.'

I drove the car at his pace. I reckoned he was around forty-five. At first sight he seemed like a fit man. He was stocky, without any fat on him. His step had a good solid spring to it. If he'd decided to run away over the hill the only way to stop him would have been to shoot him. But there were rings under his eyes and a droop to his mouth which made him look unhappy, demoralized.

Maybe I had him wrong. Maybe he wasn't frightened by us. Maybe he was depressed.

His clothes were good quality country wear: a three-piece tweed suit, a woollen cap and black leather boots. Perhaps he was one of these types who put city people off the scent. You take him for an obscure, fascinating genius: he turns out to be a schizophrenic. You take him for a schizophrenic: he turns out to own ten farms and trade horses to France on the side.

As we turned around the hill, approaching the house, I saw four horses in a paddock. Beyond that, sixty head of cattle grazing in a field. There was a yard outside the door of the house boarded by stables, sheds and a garage in which I saw a Fiat with a foreign registration: MI. 732.4117.

The house was typical of the older style you find in that part of Ireland: two storey, with a steeply angled slate roof, thick walls, small windows and wooden frames. It must have been the guts of two hundred years old. The walls had been freshly whitewashed. Inside, they were just as white. Inside, on that sunny morning, the house had a calm, light, cool atmosphere. He led us through an open doorway onto shiny grey flagstones. Verdi filled the house. Just before we entered the kitchen, which was the source of the music, the scent of fresh basil hit us.

It too had a flagstone floor. There was a long wooden table in the centre of it, on which were laid a number of dishes, including a salad bowl. That was the source of the basil. There was a bench on one side of the table, three-legged stools on the other and two big wooden chairs at either end. To our right as we entered was a large window which offered a view of fields, hills and forest with a river in the distance. To our left was an ancient wooden dresser stacked with crockery and glasses. Beside that was a door to a pantry – we could see shelves laden with bottles of wine.

Directly opposite us there was an Aga cooker, at which a woman stood with her back to us, stirring a pot, singing along to the music.

'Maria,' said the man. 'Rivoluzionarii.'

She finished stirring, lifted the pot with two hands, turned and carried it to the table where she placed it carefully on a round wooden board like a bread board. It was minestrone soup and it smelled delicious.

Maria was one of the most striking-looking women I'd ever seen. She was tall, about five-ten. She had broad shoulders which seemed hunched, even when she stood up straight above the pot to look at us. She had long, thick, glossy black hair. She had big eyes, oval and black, like olives. Her skin was very sallow, very smooth. From the centre of her face jutted a big Roman nose. Her mouth, which was also big, was open, because she was panting a little after lifting the pot. There were lots of white teeth in her mouth. She wore a white tee-shirt, loose black jeans and tennis shoes. Her breasts were huge and wonderful. They nearly made me drop my gun.

'Ecco. Rivoluzionarii,' she said, eyeing us up and down. 'Revolutionaries who lost their way.'

'We're honourable people,' I said – I was getting sick of repeating this – 'We just want to stay here for a while. If you'll just bear with us you won't come to any harm.'

Maria shrugged her shoulders and the man said nothing.

'How many people live here?' Babington inquired.

'Just me and Maria,' said the man. His accent was Irish, but I couldn't quite place it.

Stephen motioned me upstairs to check. Upstairs was of a piece with downstairs. Whitewash on the walls and ceilings, wooden furniture. There was a study with loads of books, half of them Italian. Only one bedroom appeared to be in use. It had varnished wooden floors, a great four-poster bed. It has another, even better view of the hills and fields. The thought of being in that bed with Maria made my mouth dry.

Back in the kitchen, I found Stephen, Francisco, Babington and Dermot all sitting around the table, eating soup. Their guns were on the floor beneath their places.

'You like minestrone?' said Maria to me.

'I love it.'

'Put the car in the garage,' said Stephen.

I looked to them all for some kind of explanation of what was going on. They ignored me.

'It's okay,' said Maria. 'I'm a revoluzionario too. So is Paddy.'

Here she pointed to the man, who was now standing in the doorway of the pantry, uncorking a bottle of wine. Babington and Stephen paused to turn for a closer look at him.

'You don't remember me, Stephen, but I remember you from the Curragh,' said Paddy.

'This is a good Chianti, a Broglio. Do you fancy a glass?'

'Certo,' said Stephen and Francisco together.

'Bravo,' said Maria.

I drove the car into the garage. Maria and Paddy had another car there, an Austin, and a workshop with wood, saws, a vice, hammers, nails and what have you. Some chairs were under construction. There were fishing rods, a bicycle. I looked through the window and saw an orchard with beehives. Some goats were cropping the grass at the base of the trees.

As I recrossed the yard, I heard a wild peal of laughter from Maria. The conversation around the table was humming. The Broglio was gone already. Francisco had been given the job of opening another bottle.

'This is a Frecciarossa. It's fucking beautiful stuff,' he confided. And so it proved.

'Spaghetti alla carbonara?' asked Babington, passing a dish from Maria to me.

'Beautiful.'

'Have some Parmesan,' said Stephen. 'Throw in a little

olive oil as well. That's what I do.'

'How did you get out of the Curragh?' Babington asked Paddy. 'I can't place you at all.'

'I was there alright.'

'And then you went to Italy?'

'Yeah!'

Maria downed a huge glass of Frecciarossa in one long swallow. The wine trickled from both corners of her mouth. 'Good wine!'

'Ecco!' said Paddy, somewhat less enthusiastically. Maria beamed back at him.

'Paddy! Montepulciano!' she said.

The salad had lettuce, tomato, mozzarella cheese, basil, olive oil. I'd no sooner finished mine when Maria put another dish in front of me: peas done in butter with grated onion and ham. Divine.

'Piselli alla Romana,' she said.

'What's that one like?' said Dermot, pointing to the glass Paddy had put in front of Babington.

'The Montepulciano? Excellent,' said Babington.

Dermot emptied his glass and held it out to Paddy for a refill. Soon there wasn't a lot left in that bottle either. Maria produced a big dish from the oven: kidneys stuffed with crushed nuts, parsley and fennel. There was spinach and bread rolls to go with them.

'How come you made so much food?' Babington asked, in between mouthfuls.

'People often call by,' she said.

After leaving the Curragh – Paddy didn't say exactly how he got out and we didn't ask him – he'd made his way to Rome, where Maria's father ran a restaurant in Trastevere, frequented by revolutionaries. Trouble with the police had prompted her and Paddy to come to Ireland. They didn't say how they'd got the money to buy this farm. They didn't shut out the possibility that it was all part of the revolutionary design.

For dessert we had semolina dumplings with cheese washed down by a mild white wine called Moscato.

'Well,' said Maria. 'What are your ideas?'

'That's his department,' said Stephen, pointing at Babington. 'I just organize things.'

Maria filled up Babington's glass. Not that he needed any encouragement. We were all crazy about her at that stage. If she'd wanted us to, we'd have driven back to Carlow and held up the town all over again. Then we heard the sound of an engine outside. I went upstairs for a look and saw a police car coming through the gate. We took up positions inside the door, having locked Maria and Paddy in the pantry – with a corkscrew.

'If they come through that door, we take the bastards,' said Stephen.

I prayed that the police would just drive up, turn around and go away. The food and the wine had sent us all as high as kites.

The police car drove around the yard without stopping and went back the way they came.

Our first reaction was relief. Then anxiety. What if they'd spotted something? They might return and surround the place.

I asked Paddy to show me on the map how to get to Aughrim in County Wicklow by marching across the mountains. He described various routes. You could go Graney – Rathvilly – Kiltegan – Hackettstown. Or you could go via Ballon, crossing the Slaney at Tullow, then take the road to Shillelagh and Tinahely. Paddy was from the area. He'd walked the roads and hills with his father and grandfather. He knew the history, the folklore, the people, everything.

When we returned to the kitchen, Babington was in full flight, explaining his ideas to Maria, over cappuccinos.

The internees had spent a lot of time discussing the reasons why their campaign hadn't got very far. Some felt the movement had attracted no popular support because it was not grounded in the day-to-day experience of ordinary people: poverty, unemployment, emigration, social stagnation. What was wanted was a broad-based socialist movement linking up with the international socialist revolutionary movement. Others said the reason they hadn't won popular support was that they'd botched up so many military operations. As an army, they lacked credibility. Why should the masses flock to the ranks of such an incompetent outfit?

Babington agreed with Gramsci that revolutionaries sometimes over-stressed the importance of economic matters. If they were so important, why hadn't there been revolutions in all the countries where the working-class cause was well developed? The struggle between competing classes was conducted at a variety of levels. Ireland's problem, like that of many other countries, was essentially one of colonialism. In this the role of culture was crucial. It was an area where consciousness could be triggered.

Sculpture was a point of intersection between colonialism and culture. Through sculpture, the ideology of previous eras survived into the present. It was amenable to physical assault. Through attacking sculpture, you could strike a blow for intellectual freedom.

85

The object was to root out colonialism from the Irish consciousness. The first step in the campaign would be to mount a series of attacks upon memorials to Irish colonialists and the colonialist work of Foley, the Irish sculptor. Military targets would have priority. He, Babington, was drawing up a list of possibilities, together with profiles of the subjects involved, initially for consideration by the group, but also with an eye to publicity in the immediate aftermath of the attacks, which would be timed to occur in various countries within the space of a few days. He was confident that the attacks would be warmly welcomed by those involved in the anti-colonialist struggle throughout the world and that the response would stimulate an enlarged campaign

'It's a good idea,' said Maria. 'I like this idea.'

'It has a certain flavour,' said Paddy.

I asked him for the number plates and tax disc of their Irish car. He wasn't very happy about this, but could hardly refuse, having made an offer of assistance. He felt better about it when we gave him some money.

TEN

FOLEY'S CONTEMPORARIES reckoned that his finest works were the three equestrian statues which stood upon the Maidan in Calcutta, the memorials to Viscount Hardinge, Earl Canning and Sir James Outram. If the finest horse was Hardinge's, the outstanding human figure was that of Outram, 'the Bayard of India'.

Ye who have joyed to read, in Spenser's lay,
How, in old time, a champion pure did ride,
Through twilight wood, at 'heavenly Una's' side,
Guarding the meek one on her dangerous way;
Ye who lament o'er past romance today,
Here see portrayed, a 'knight of holiness'
Prompt to redeem the helpless in distress,
And for the weak his lance in rest to lay,
Bayard Of India! No reproach or fear

Stained thy bright scutcheon. Nor alone in fight
Pre-eminent wert thou, but could'st forbear
Valour's high guerdon, quit thy lawful right,
And bid a comrade's brow thy laurels wear;
Thus manifest in all 'a perfect Knight'.

Not that the Outram horse is an inferior work. It's carved in the attitude of a sudden rearing, on account of the rider drawing the reins. The animal has been pulled backwards onto its hind legs, which are nearly bent in two under the weight they are supporting. The left foreleg is straight, touching the ground at an angle of 45 degrees. The right foreleg is bent double and raised high in the air. The head gives an impression of terror: the jaw has been wrenched wide open, the nostrils are flaring and the eyes are bulging and wide. The tail juts out at right angles to the buttocks, thereby contributing to the impression of the gallop being suddenly arrested.

The movement has been stopped short because the rider has turned in the saddle to look at something behind him. He holds the reins in his left hand and a sword in his right. The sword-arm is held low, the tip beneath the hilt, as though he were preparing to parry rather than strike a blow. Apart from a few tassels on his chest and a sash around the waist, Outram's attire is workaday, inglorious. The jacket, trousers and boots are drab, worn, dusty.

The face is that of a man in late middle age. His hair is receding from his forehead in front and, at the sides, covering his ears in two shaggy bunches. His moustache is long and thick. His cheeks are wrinkled and bumpy. The eyes look tired and puffy, the skin beneath them is lined. Of beard, all there is is a puff of hair beneath the lower lip. Thin at the bridge, the nose broadens around the nostrils. The brow is furrowed. The right eyebrow is straight, the left arched.

It's not the face of an aristocrat, a Wellesley, an Ellenborough, a Dalhousie or a Canning. It's the face of your everyday middle-class man, a grafter, a man of immense practical experience. What's noble in Outram is his gaze: calm, penetrating, fearless. The shoulders are slightly hunched, the head is slightly bent. Not someone born to nobility, but one who made or earned it for himself.

Why is he not portrayed looking forward, like Gough or Hardinge? Foley researched the lives of his subjects in detail before he set to work. As well as achieving a likeness of the physique and features, he sought to capture or express the essence of the subject's character, to carve in stone the qualities which he, and of course those who had commissioned the work, considered ideal and worthy of commemoration. In Outram, the backward turn stands for thoughtfulness, reflection. This is a moral man. His strength and capacity is coupled with integrity. His strength and energy were the qualities needful for winning and keeping an empire. His goodness made the enterprise seem, not merely justifiable, but desirable.

Violence and peacefulness, severity and lenity, were evident in Outram's character from his earliest campaigns, nowhere more so than in his encounter with the Bhils. These wildest of wild men had lived for centuries in the hills and jungles of Khandesh, surviving by hunting and by raiding the villages of their neighbours. The consensus among those who were not Bhils was that the best way of dealing with them was to shoot them dead whenever an opportunity presented itself. Then Mountelphinstone Stuart, the wise old Governor of Bombay, struck out upon a different tack. He determined to turn the Bhils into farmers and soldiers. To Outram, at the tender age of twenty-two, was entrusted the soldiering part of this new policy.

To begin with, the Bhils showed little inclination to change their ways. Indeed they showed little inclination even to speak to Outram. They forced him to resort to terror.

One dark night he gathered together whatever troops he could muster, which amounted to no more than thirty bayonets. Already adept at intelligence-gathering, the young Scot had enlisted the services of a spy, who led his party to the mountain-stronghold of the Bhils. The wild men were completely taken by surprise. They scattered in all directions, abandoning their women and children to Outram, in the belief that the entire British army was upon them. Now Outram divided his men into bands of three and four to pursue them, before they had a chance to rally and see the small number of redcoats with which they were faced. They could hear gunfire from everywhere, soldiers running in all directions. The pursuit continued through the night and next day Outram brought in reinforcements. It continued for days ...

Outram released certain of his captives with a view to bringing in the fugitives on his personal pledge that all should be set free. The Bhils now saw that Outram was a man of his word. They saw that he had the courage to place his trust in them, something no man had ever done before. For months, completely unguarded, Outram lived among the wild men. He hunted with the hunters ...

Outram was the outstanding hunter of his day in India and there have been few to rival him since. His shikar-book for the seasons 1822–23 and 1823–24 at Rajkat records that he claimed seventy-four of one hundred and twenty-three 'first-spears' won by a party of twelve. In addition he killed four nilgai (obtained in seven runs at the cost of four horses), two hyenas and two wolves. Small wonder that it was in the realm of the chase that Outram made further strong impression upon the sensibilities of the wild Bhil. A few of the many tales of his adventures will suffice to illustrate the point. He and his Bhils were chasing a cheetah around the Nandurbar Hills. The cheetah hid in a cave at the side of a hill which was too deep for a human to descend. The wild men were stumped. Not so Outram. He instructed the Bhil to remove their putrees and tie them together to form a rope. He tied one end around his waist and bid them lower him into the cave. There he killed the cheetah. Once on a tiger-hunt he descended from his elephant to wait, spear in hand, outside a large earth into which a wounded tiger had fled. At last the animal emerged and Outram thrust the spear at its neck. But the tiger brushed the weapon aside with ease and loped off. On another occasion, a wounded tiger having escaped into its lair which was covered by long reeds, Outram followed it in on his hands and knees.

Even the Bhils felt that this was pushing courage to the point of foolhardiness. Happily, the tiger ran away when it caught wind of Outram's approach. This was the spirit which produced, by 1833, a ten-year tally of one hundred and ninety-one tigers, twenty-five bears, fifteen leopards and twelve buffaloes, all killed.

The Bhils were somewhat bemused by Outram's bravado in the bath-tub. Once, when bathing in a tank, he was told that a friend had jumped from the top of the bathhouse, which was two storeys high. Outram ordered the steps of the house to be placed upon the roof, and jumped from them. Then he ordered that a savage young alligator be put in the tank. Outram entered the water with the reptile, and bathed. On another occasion, near Sindwa, he decided to jump off a wall into a tank, using an umbrella as a parachute. He had, however, miscalculated the capacity of the umbrella to sustain his weight and the instrument fell asunder in mid-leap. Happily, he was not seriously injured and spent only a short time under water.

It was not long before Outram persuaded five chief men of the Bhil to walk the path of civilization by becoming the first recruits in his new battalion. The new corps was made to feel welcome by men of the highest caste from long-established regiments, who presented the Bhil recruits with Betel nut. Within a year three hundred and three moved into barracks. Those in the hills gave up strong liquor and ceased raiding their neighbours. They bought grinding stones and other articles for household use. In due course the corps was entrusted with the task of escorting the civil governor upon his tour of the province. (The Bombay government, while ticking him off for the violence of his measures, were pleased by Outram's results.) What was described as a miracle of moral and social regeneration received its acid test when an insurrection of rebellious Bhils afforded the new corps an opportunity of shedding their blood on behalf of their new masters. In the event, the recruits fought spiritedly against their own caste and relations.

Outram's loyalty as a friend and colleague was illustrated by his defence of Lieutenant Hammersley, whom some in authority wished to make the scapegoat for an Afghan set-back. As Nott retired to Peshawar via Ghazni and Kabul, General England led the spare troops, guns and stores to Quetta, en route to Sind. Before he reached Kandahar, England was put to flight by a small bunch of tribesmen who his troops should have routed with no difficulty. England claimed Hammersley had failed to warn him of the tribesmen's movements ... Outram suffered from one of his periodic bouts of brain fever on account of the stress he experienced attending Hammersley's sickbed. Government ordered that Hammersley be dismissed from 'political' employment. Outram refused to comply with the order, saying that Hammersley was never more badly needed. Even after Hammersley's death, which doctors attributed to this unjust treatment, Outram continued to plead the cause of his friend. He himself recovered, and went on to lead a party of Brahui horsemen guarding England's progress through the Bolan Pass. This did not soothe attitudes to Outram's insubordination and he was himself dismissed from the political service when his mission was complete.

Like Nicholson and many another distinguished officer, Outram had lost his father when he was a boy. Doubtless this fact influenced his acceptance of the charge of the dying Emir of Hyderbad, Nur Mohammed. Outram had been appointed Political Agent for the lower Sind in 1840, and his efforts quickly bore fruit. Taxes on produce brought to the British camp at Karachi were reduced; tolls were reduced on Indus traffic. There was a new, improved treaty with Mirpur. It was due to Outram's personal influence that Nur Mohammed Khan gave up his mistrust of British policy and became a friend. 'From the days of Adam no one has known so great truth and friendship as I have found in you,' said the dying Khan. Some days later he took the hands of his brother Nasir Khan and his younger son Husain Ali and placed them in Outram's hands saying, 'You are their father and brother, you will protect them.'

Sir Charles Napier succeeded Outram as the architect of British policy in Sind when Outram was dismissed from political service. Napier quickly undermined the trust and mutual understanding which Outram had carefully fostered. Outram criticized these new policies which oppressed the Emirs. The people of Sind eventually revolted against the British, but Napier crushed them at the battle of Miani (the name Viscount Hardinge gave his charger). Outram was thoroughly disgusted by the whole business. He found Husain Ali Khan's name on a list of rebels due for execution after the battle. He interceded on his behalf, 'out of respect for his late father', and Husain Ali was set free. Outram's share of the Sind prize-money amounted to £3000. He refused to keep this money, choosing instead to distribute it among charities.

Napier it was, however, who orchestrated Outram's rehabilitation following the Hammersley affair. He said he was much obliged to him for the information which was his bequest. He proposed Outram's health at a public dinner at Sakhar on November the 5th, 1842: 'Gentlemen, I give you the "Bayard of India", *sans peur et sans reproche*, Major James Outram of the Bombay army.' Henceforth, Outram was Bayard.

But who was Bayard?

He was Pierre Terrail, *seigneur de Bayard, le chevalier sans peur et sans reproche*, the knight without fear and without reproach, who was born near Pontcherra in France about 1473. He was part of Charles VIII's expedition into Italy in 1494 and knighted for his action at Fornovo the following year. He distinguished himself in many combats during the reign of Louis XII. He defended the bridge over the Garighano single-handed against two hundred Spaniards. In 1508 he gave outstanding service at the siege of Genoa and afterwards at the siege of Padua. Despite the wounds he received at Brescia, he took part in the battle of Ravenna in 1512.

Francis I succeeded to the throne of France in 1515 and appointed Bayard General of Dauphine. With just 1000 men he held Mézières against the forces of Charles V, the Holy Roman Emperor, some 35,000 troops. This action enabled the King to raise the army which drove out the invaders. His last campaign was in Italy, where he was wounded defending the retreat at Sesia of the defeated army of Guillaume de Bonnevet.

Mariette's engraving of Bayard shows a man in late middle age. He wears a suit of armour, with the helmet resting on a table at his right hand. In his left he holds his lance. He has a long moustache and a curly beard, with the same puff of hair beneath the lower lip that Outram has. He has a full crop of hair and the same furrowed brow as Outram. He too glances sideways, or backwards, and is rendered meditative thereby. The lips are pursed, the eyebrows arched. The gaze is penetrating, assured. You don't want to have to fight this guy – certainly not in single combat. His nose bespeaks the nobleman born: long, straight, rounded at the nostrils. Neither proud nor contemptuous, just superior.

The Hammersley affair and its consequences by no means signalled the end of Outram's willingness to break a lance with authorities in the interests of truth as he saw it. When appointed political agent in Baroda, he immediately set himself against the khatpat – corruption – which was rife in the administration of the province. Despite his bringing to the notice of the Bombay government a mountain of evidence against a series of individuals including public officials, his efforts to root out evil won no support in that quarter. Outram instituted a series of prosecutions himself. He went over the heads of the Bombay government by presenting a report to the court of directors in Leadenhall Street, a course of action which resulted in his removal from office, as he expected it would. The Board subsequently endorsed the stand he had taken. Many attempts were made upon his life at this time. Someone put poison in his hookah. This brought on the 'mysterious illness' which necessitated his travelling to Egypt to convalesce.

It was there in the desert that for the one and only time in his life – and just for ten minutes – he met Henry and Honoria Lawrence, as they hurried to India to try to prevent the outbreak in the Punjab from becoming the Second Sikh War.

Outram never enjoyed a stage like that of Waterloo or Gujerat on which to display his outstanding soldierly abilities. Those who suspected his diplomatic initiatives of weakness simply because he did his best to effect reconciliation were often alarmed at the ferocity he displayed when he took the gloves off. Thus he rejected Sir Robert Grant's policy of leniency towards the troublesome Mahi Kanta. He believed that men are never in a better mood to listen to your reason, and to appreciate your kindness, than after you have well beaten them: 'Demonstrate your power over them and they will respect your mediation, appreciate your clemency.' He proclaimed the insurgent Surj Mall an outlaw and pursued him relentlessly until he and his associate chiefs were crying for mercy. Once more, the government's praise was tempered by cries of 'foul!' for aspects of the campaign he conducted and allegations of excessive violence being employed.

Outram had consistently counselled against the government's Afghan policy and predicted its collapse although even he, as he later confessed, could not have foreseen that 5000 British troops would commit suicide. There was a curious prelude to the campaign. En route to Kandahar, his Cutch camel drivers went on strike.

Outram's approach to the problem would scarcely meet the approval of a modern labour-relations consultant, but it was nevertheless effective. One driver was tied down and given two dozen lashes; a second was tied and given three dozen lashes; a third was given four dozen lashes. After that the strikers went back to work and promised obedience. Outram arrived in Kabul in time to witness the installation of Shah Shuja, the so-called 'rightful heir to the throne'. Outram was not surprised to see the lack of enthusiasm for the new leader on the part of the people of Kabul, who stayed away from the celebrations in large numbers. This in no way deterred his spirited pursuit of the deposed Emir, Dost Mohammed, which was foiled only by the treacherous manoeuvrings of Hay Khan, commander of Shah Shuja's cavalry. He pacified the territory between Kabul and Kandahar, capturing and demolishing many forts. At Ghazni, six hundred of the enemy were slain. Disguised as an Afghan, surviving only on dates and water, he explored the route from Kalat to Sommiani.

The single outstanding exploit of his career from a military point of view occurred during his second stint in Sind, when Napier appointed him commissioner for the purpose of revising the treaty with the Emirs (who were complaining that their livelihoods had been taken away, they'd nothing more to give). On the 14th of February, 1843, Outram defended his residence at Haidarabad from an attack of 8000 Beluchis led by Mir Shahdad Khan.

The company's residence was a square enclosure skirted on three sides by a wall barely five feet high. The fourth side looked upon the river, from which the company's steamer *The Planet* could fire her twelve-pound gun at the Beluchis. The garrison, commanded by Captain Conway, consisted of no more than a hundred men. For three hours they withstood the attack of 8000. Ammunition was running low. The enemy were moving guns into position. Then another company steamer, *The Satellite*, came on the scene, but with no men aboard and no cartridges. It was time to retire. At a signal, those in the front of the company fell back into the residency. All the baggage was stowed aboard in an hour. The retreat sounded. All posts but one were left. Conway marched the men in sections to the steamer. The last defenders dropped from the windows of the building to cover this movement. In the entire engagement Outram lost only three killed and twelve wounded as against sixty dead and four times the number wounded of the enemy.

Sir Charles Napier praised the action as a 'brilliant example of how to defend a military post'. He had himself just won the battle of Miani, in which the enemy lost 5000 killed at the cost of only 19 officers and 256 men. (It was one of the outstanding victories of Indian military history, and accomplished the annexation of Sind.)

In 1857 Outram was given command of an army charged with disputing the Persian claim to Herat in Afghanistan. He landed at Bushahr on the 27th of January and immediately set out to attack the Persian camp at Barozjan. He arrived to discover that the enemy had abandoned the camp with all its stores. The following day, however, he was attacked by 6000 Persians at Khushab. Outram put them to flight, killing 600. Gales delayed the next step in the campaign, an attack on Muhamra. Once the troops landed the Persians did not contest matters for long – they exploded their largest magazine and fled. But by now the war was over, for peace talks were arranged at Baghdad.

Although he was exhausted, the last and most famous action of Outram's career lay before him upon his return to India, namely the relief of Lucknow in the province of Oudh, whose annexation he had himself effected two years previously.

Banner of England, not for a season, oh banner of Britain hast thou
Floated in conquering battle or flapt to the battle-cry!

*Never with mightier glory than when we had rear'd thee on
  high*
Flying at top of the roofs in the ghastly siege of Lucknow –
*Shot thro' the staff or the halyard, but ever we raised thee
  anew,*
And ever upon the topmost roof our banner of England blew.

Outram surrendered his rank to General Havelock and
joined him as a volunteer, so that Havelock would have to
himself the glory of the relief of the city. He was at first
praised for magnanimity, then criticized for casting aside
the burden of responsibility when the scale of the casual-
ties suffered by Havelock became apparent. It was suggested that Outram had given up the command because
he wanted to win the Victoria Cross and feared that he
would be disqualified from winning it by virtue of his
seniority.

*Hark cannode, fusillade! Is it true what was told by the
  scout,*
*Outram and Havelock breaking their way through the fell
  mutineers?*
Surely the pibroch of Europe is ringing again in our ears
All on a sudden the garrison utter a jubilant shout,
*Havelock's glorious Highlanders answer with conquering
  cheers*
*Sick from the hospital echo them, women and children come
  out,*
*Blessing the wholesome white faces of Havelock's good fusil-
  liers,*
*Kissing the war-hardened hand of the Highlander wet with
  their tears!*

Outram, the chief commissioner for Oudh, resumed command once installed in the residency. He found, however, that for the moment he had reinforced the garrison rather than raised the siege. For that he had to wait until the arrival in November of Sir Colin Campbell.

The problem was to make contact with Campbell. Thomas Kavanagh, a Limerickman working as a clerk in the company's service in Lucknow, persuaded Outram to let him attempt to make the vital communication. Disguised as a native, Kavanagh slipped from the Residency at dead of night. The streets of the town were swarming with armed men and the countryside was bristling with pickets ... Early in the morning a 'very peculiar-looking individual' presented himself to a British outpost. Kavanagh was taken to Campbell and gave Sir Colin verbal messages, the city plan, a code of signals and a letter pointing out the easiest road to use. Now Outram and Campbell could liaise. Twenty-four hours later Campbell destroyed Fort Jalalabad and captured the Sikandrabagh. Outram, the same day, blew in the outer wall of Farid Baksh's palace, opened batteries on rebel defences and stormed the steam-engine house. He made his way to Campbell with a small party of officers.

Sir Colin entrusted to Outram the evacuation of the garrison to Diklusha. This he accomplished with great skill along the bank of the Gumti during the night of the 22nd of September. The success of the manoeuvre was marred by the loss of Havelock, whose last moments on the 23rd Outram shared. Outram carved a cross upon the mango tree beneath which Havelock was buried.

Sir Colin called upon Outram for one final, magnificent effort. Like Bayard with his 1000 holding Mézières against the 35,000 of Charles V, now Outram was charged with checking the Lucknow mutineers, some 120,000 men with 130 guns led by the redoubtable maulvi, Ahmad Shah. Outram and his 5000 took up a position on the road to Cawnpore, surrounding it with trenches, batteries and constructions of different kinds. They managed to survive prolonged harassment and a series of bitter and deadly engagements until Sir Colin reappeared on the 1st of March.

Honours flooded upon him. The queen made him a baronet. Parliament voted him an annuity of £1000.

In 1859 Robert Montgomery replaced Outram as Chief Commissioner of Oudh, while Sir James became military member of the government's council. But the great effort had taken its toll. In 1860 his health collapsed. He returned to England, leaving behind the bulk of his property, including his library, for the use of the soldiers. (He kept Froissart's *Chronicles* and the *Life of Bayard*.) He travelled to France and Egypt, vainly seeking to recover his health. In Alexandria he briefly encountered the broken Canning, en route to London and death. Neither had much heart for discussion, especially upon the issue of the confiscation of the lands of the rebellious talukdars of Oudh, which had occupied them so much in 1858. Outram, supported by Campbell, attended their old leader's funeral in Westminster Abbey, little realizing that he would himself be buried beside Canning the following year. Mourners were moved by the presence of ordinary Highland soldiers, come to bury their chief, among the hosts of dignitaries. And one or two black faces were present also.

Praise to our Indian brothers, and let the dark face have his
due!
Thanks to the kindly dark faces who fought with us, faith-
ful and few,
Fought with the bravest among us, and drove them, and
smote them, and slew,
That ever upon the topmost roof our banner in India blew.

As a child, Outram had shown inclination to be a sculptor. He loved to carve figures with his pen-knife out of any materials he could lay his hands on. He would visit the menageries which came to Aberdeen and carve all the animals he saw, especially the monkeys whose comic attitudes he learned to represent very effectively. His mother considered sculpting as a career for him but, 'having no friends in that line, did not make any endeavour to follow up this view'. His best piece was an elephant, carved from wood, which stood for years upon the family mantelpiece, winning the admiration of all who saw it.

ELEVEN

HENRY LAWRENCE represented the poetry of Indian statesmanship, John its hard direct prose.*

Their father Major Lawrence – the son of a mill-owner from Coleraine – served twenty-five years in India, where lack of influence hampered his advancement in the forces, although the Commander-in-Chief twice recommended his promotion. Forced into retirement by poor health and the effects of the wounds he had suffered, Major Lawrence was granted only one third of the pension to which he was entitled by the rules of service. Lord Palmerston, Secretary of State for War, coldly rejected his request to be paid the full amount. The outlook for the

* This analogy made by Captain Trotter in his life of John Lawrence.

young Lawrences seemed bleak until the East India Company increased the money to a figure nearer the mark, a gesture which greatly relieved their mother Emily, a wonderful woman from Donegal, daughter of the Reverend George Knox who boasted a slight but genuine connection with John Knox, the reformer.

John Lawrence said of his first school in Bristol, where everyone called him Paddy, that 'he was flogged every day except one, when he was flogged twice'. He said of his second school, Foyle College in Derry, where his mother's brother Jimmy was headmaster, that he 'did not learn very much'. He did, however, learn a little about sieges. There was a field near the college where the boarders had built a fortress. This had to be defended at all hours of the day and night from the day boys. Henry and John were leading lights among the boarders whose motto was, predictably, 'no surrender'.

Although he wanted to follow his elder brothers George, Alexander and Henry into the army, John was persuaded by his sister Letitia to opt instead for the civil service. The pay was better in the civil service. When he went to India he would contribute a portion of his salary to 'the Lawrence fund', established by the older boys for the purpose of supporting their mother and younger siblings at home. It was, however, with something less than wholehearted enthusiasm that John attended the service training-school, Haileybury College. The principal complained that his son was 'loafing about with that tall Irishman instead of sticking to more regular students'. The professor of maths did not think him a good student, but 'forgave him on account of his Orange zeal and fun'.

He completed his training at Fort William College in Calcutta. Then he was appointed assistant judge, magistrate and collector of the city of Delhi and its environs, an area with a population of five million. His rise in the service was slow but steady. After four years in Delhi and two in Paniput, he was promoted to Acting-Magistrate and Collector for the district of Gurgaon.

Tax-collection was Lawrence's forte. A village of defaulters once awoke to discover that he and his police were surrounding them, blocking the path to the pasture. The villagers did nothing, hoping that Lawrence would go away after a few hours. But he didn't go away. The cattle moaned from hunger. Finally the villagers gave in and handed over the money. On another occasion he stood for hours in the hot season outside the gate of a big landowner. The headman of a neighbouring village volunteered support by standing his men alongside Lawrence. At this the landowner paid up.

He was an excellent detective. The murdered body of Ram Singh was found late one night on a sandy piece of ground. Lawrence used a torch to examine the pattern of footprints in the vicinity. He grasped that Ram Singh had been attacked by a group of people, one of whom had raced around the victim to drive him towards the others. Lawrence knew that Ram Singh was a fast runner, so this man must have been very fast indeed. Lawrence also knew that Bulram Singh, the victim's brother, was a postman – postmen were chosen for their running ability.

Moreover, he knew the brothers had quarrelled. He found Bulram smoking quietly in his room. But his heart, on which Lawrence placed a hand, was beating fast. And there was blood on his groin. 'Yes, I killed him,' Bulram said. He was hanged shortly afterwards.

When his friend William Fraser was murdered, Lawrence followed the trail of a horse from the scene of the crime. The trail ended abruptly at a cross-roads. He learned that the Nawab of Ferozepore had born a grudge against Fraser. He found the Nawab's horse in the yard of his house and noticed nailmarks in the hoofs in unusual places. He remembered that, to deceive pursuers, Dick Turpin would shoe his horses backwards. The Nawab too was hanged shortly afterwards.

Lawrence early learned the value of resolute action in a crisis. During a famine in the town of Rewari, Moslems proposed to eat oxen. Hindus regarded this as an insult to their religion and threatened force to prevent it. Then they hit upon the Irish tactic of the boycott. Hindu shopkeepers refused to sell food to Moslems. Lawrence set up a food supply of his own by organizing the distribution of grain through selected retailers. This effectively smashed the boycott for the Hindu traders, when they realized that they faced ruin to no purpose.

In 1849 Lawrence returned from India on furlough. He professed himself to be in search of a wife, whom he called 'the calamity'. He found one very like his mother, a clergyman's daughter from Donegal. Harriet Catherine Hamilton's father was the rector of Guldaff and Cloncha. As testimony of the regard in which the Hamiltons were held by the local community, rich and poor, Catholic and Protestant, mighty and humble, all flocked to the wedding. Unfortunately the couple's honeymoon was cut short by the news that George Lawrence was a prisoner in Kabul. Although not yet recovered from the effects of Etawa fever, Lawrence hastened to India.

He arrived to find the war over, George released and Henry's star high in the ascendant on account of the role he had played in the affair.

John's steady progress continued. He was appointed Civil and Sessions Judge in Delhi. Then he took charge at Kurnal, a district afflicted by plague. He identified swamps used to grow rice as the source of the evil and quickly put matters to rights. Next he was appointed Magistrate and Collector of Delhi and Paniput.

Major Lawrence had impressed upon his sons that the reason for the straitened circumstances of their childhood was his own lack of influence. Influence was the key to real advancement in India. They would have to win it. John's opportunity to do that presented itself in the shape of Sir Henry Hardinge. The Governor-General's preparation for conflict with the Sikhs naturally included an appraisal of the situation along the frontier. This meant meeting John Lawrence. Hardinge was greatly impressed by the younger man's energy and resourcefulness. When the Khalsa crossed the Sutlej, Hardinge gave out his famous order: 'Send me John Lawrence!'

Now Lawrence was given a task of crucial importance, organizing supplies for Gough's army. Since traditionally the supplying of the Indian armies had been a nightmare of mismanagement – Henry had been obliged to borrow guns from the Sikhs on behalf of the Afghan relief force – a Hercules was required. And a Hercules was what John Lawrence proved himself to be. The war hung in the balance until Sobraon. That battle was determined by the arrival of an enormous supply train. To put this on the road he had to single-handedly overhaul the whole system of raising and distributing supplies. He had to devise a means of fairly compensating property owners for their losses. He not only hired some 7000 drivers and their servants, but raised morale among them to the point where, en route, there were scarcely any desertions. Thus 4000 carts, drawn by 29,000 oxen, arrived at Gough's camp.

Two incidents from this period show that the Foyle College Hercules was not without his lighter and human side. He and a number of others were crushed into a howdah on the back of an elephant, going through the streets of Lahore. Lawrence spotted an elephant approaching, with just a single officer on board. He persuaded a young subaltern to relieve the space by jumping across to the oncoming elephant where a 'nice old gentleman would welcome him with open arms'. The young man did as he was told, but had to grab the old gentleman around the neck to prevent himself from falling. The 'nice old gentleman' proved to be Colonel Stuart, Military Secretary to the Government of India, who, on hearing the explanation of what had happened, roared: 'I'll pay off Master John for this!' After the treaty was signed, Lawrence was given custody of the Koh-I-Nur pending its carriage to London. One day, in council, he was instructed to transfer the diamond to an officer. Lawrence realized, to mounting horror, that he could not remember where he had put it. He said nothing except that he would keep the appointment with the officer the following day. He feared that he was ruined. His fellow officers and officials and immediate superiors would take his word that he had made a mistake, but in the public domain a stigma would forever attach to his name. There would always be the suspicion that he had misappropriated the jewel, the cause of more than one war and the corruption of countless persons. He would be obliged to withdraw from public life. Happily, the Koh-I-Nur turned up in the pocket of a suit which a servant had collected for cleaning.

Hardinge rewarded his outstanding service in the campaign by appointing him Governor of the newly annexed province of Jalandar Doab. This fertile and well-populated territory had been one of the most productive regions of the Sikh kingdom. Lawrence set about making it more productive. To begin with, he reduced the tax burden on the cultivators of the soil and in the process substituted cash tax payments for payments in kind. He built roads, canals, bridges. He reformed the administration of justice. He endeavoured to curb barbarous practices, like the murder of female infants, the burning of widows upon their husbands' funeral pyres, the burning of lepers. The stature he achieved among the population in a short space of time was confirmed by their response to his reaction to the outbreak at Multan. He toured the province, summoning the men of Jalandar Doab to a series of assemblies. He called upon each man to step up to the table at which he sat, on which were laid a pen and a sword. 'How do you wish to be ruled?' he asked. 'By the pen or the sword?' All of them grasped the pen.

After Gujerat, Lawrence became one of the triumvirs who formed the Punjab Board of Administration. This was perhaps the most outstanding government of its kind the world has seen. His personal responsibilities were finance and administration. He extended to the Punjab as a whole the reduction of taxes he had applied in Jalandar

Doab. Encouraged by the prospect of a better return for their labours, farmers produced more. The overall tax yield increased. Within three years the Punjab produced a net surplus to the central exchequer of one million sterling. He extended the Trunk Road from Delhi to Peshawar, a distance of seven hundred miles. He built a great highway from Lahore to Multan. He added one thousand miles to the Bari Doab Canal, an immense benefit to cultivators. Waste lands were reclaimed. Trees were planted. Forests were preserved. Improved breeds of cattle were introduced, along with tobacco, cotton, tea and sugarcane.

On Christmas Day 1851 a celebrated episode occurred when the three Foyle College old boys who formed the Punjab Board – Henry and John Lawrence and Robert Montgomery – ate dinner together. Henry recalled the Simpsons, brothers who had been ushers at the school for very many years. He reckoned that they could not be well off. He proposed that each of the three should contribute fifty pounds and send the lot to the Simpsons as 'a Christmas box from a far-off land with the good wishes of three of their old pupils'. George Lawrence, political agent at Nejwar, contributed fifty pounds also. The reply, when at length it arrived, was almost illegible 'from the writer's tears'. The Simpsons expressed their deepest gratitude for money which would ease the burden of their declining years, but more especially for having been remembered by former pupils who had, it seemed, risen to high positions. They confessed, however, that they did not know what the Punjab Board of Administration meant, nor had they been able to find either Punjab or Lahore in the school atlas.

The idyll did not last forever. Long-standing differences between John and Henry hardened into division. At bottom, Henry wished to adapt British ways to Indian needs, John to adapt Indians to British ways. Henry believed the administration system should be personal and flexible, John that there should be a system that was independent of individual personalities. John reckoned the Jaghurdirs – a rural aristocracy – were parasites who ought to be got rid of without delay. Henry felt that they were worthy of respect as the leaders of their society. If they were not to be preserved, they should be let down gradually, as potentially they were a disaffected and dangerous group. Robert Montgomery was often called upon to mediate between the two brothers. But each case referred to the Governor-General, Dalhousie, was decided by him in favour of John's position. When finally he abolished the Board of Administration, Dalhousie sent Henry to Rajputana and made John Governor of the Punjab.

How vast and lonely a place the Punjab now seemed to John! To sustain their family with the Lawrence fund he and his brothers had crossed the seas. Now here was a rupture between himself and Henry, his childhood idol, because they could not see eye-to-eye on the issue of the Jaghurdirs! In finding the thread which would tie the Punjab fast, he had loosened the thread which bound Henry to himself.

With Henry gone, John softened. He adopted some of his brother's policies. He made a series of favourable recommendations respecting the claims of Jaghurdirs, many of which Dalhousie turned down on the grounds that they were over-generous. He started to make use of the social system of the villages, according chief men responsibility in finance and administration. A problem was that many subordinates, who owed their positions to Henry, were unwilling to transfer their loyalties to his brother. The chief culprit was Nicholson, who showed his resentment by cutting procedural corners in a provocative way. One of his ploys was to send batches of men to Lahore for hanging without sufficient explanation. 'Don't send up any more men to be hanged direct unless the case is very urgent,' Lawrence wrote to him. 'When you do, send an abstract of the evidence in English, through the commissioner.' Nicholson would not settle down, however, and was ultimately transferred to Peshawar at his own request.

In 1853 Lawrence made a tour of inspection of the frontier. Hearing that the Afridi had reverted to their old habits of raiding and plundering, he seized an opportunity to indulge his boyhood passion for soldiering. He himself put together a raiding party which gave the Afridi a thrashing at their stronghold in the Bori Hills. When Dalhousie learned that Lawrence had met a native chieftain who had never before seen a European, he praised him for presenting himself as 'the first specimen of the conquering race'.

As a child he had suffered from ophthalmia. This meant spending a year in the dark at the age of six, learning to distinguish the presence of his mother and sisters by the shape of their hands. Now, due to the enormous pressure of work, he could feel the blindness creep up on him again. He had not had a holiday for fifteen years. He longed to retire.

He was at Rawalpindi when the Sepoys murdered the English officers at Meerut, then marched to Delhi to proclaim Dahadur Shah Emperor of Hindustan.

It was essential to send an army to Delhi. Practically speaking, that army had to come from the Punjab, which contained more British troops than Oudh, the only alternative possibility. But the risks were enormous. If the European troops withdrew, would the Pathans descend from the mountains? How would the irregulars react? If they revolted, the British would surely be overwhelmed. And what of the Punjabi peasants? Scarcely ten years ago they had formed the mighty Khalsa. Might they not seize this opportunity to reform? Would Dost Mohammed keep to the terms of his treaty? Or would the Lion of Kabul pounce to reclaim his beloved Peshawar?

Lawrence sent several European regiments to Delhi from the frontier, replacing them with Sepoy regiments which had been divided up. The protected Sikh states of Patiala, Jhind, Nabla and Kapurthala sent him men and money. He raised levies among the Punjabi peasants, exploiting to the full their resentment of Sepoy arrogance towards the defeated Khalsa. Many Jaghurdirs, on whose behalf Henry had successfully lobbied, furnished the new regiments with men and money. Thus was the Great Trunk Road patrolled and communications maintained between Lahore and Delhi.

But the situation at Delhi quickly became critical. The rebels were reinforced in far greater numbers than the besiegers. Illness pervaded the British camp. No fewer than three commanders had to be replaced on account of it. There was talk of retiring from the position.

Now Lawrence faced the most momentous decision of his life. As news of the uncertainty at Delhi spread, tension rose in the Punjab. If Lawrence chose to commit more resources to the siege, his position in the Punjab was weakened – and insurrection in the Punjab would inevitably attend failure at Delhi. On the other hand, success at Delhi would strangle the mutiny. Lawrence chose to fight in Delhi. He sent 3000 men to the siege and put together a huge supply-train.

One consequence of the crisis was the restoration of goodwill between the Foyle College old boy and Nicholson, the Royal College, Dungannon past-pupil. Nicholson and Edwards persuaded General Read to cede his military authority to Lawrence. Lawrence approved their idea of blasting the Naushera mutineers from the guns and he also gave the go-ahead to their wish to form a flying-column. With it, Nicholson struck the Sialkot mutineers upon an island in the Ravi river, slaughtering nearly all 1100 of their number. Lawrence ordered him at the head of the column to the siege, where their arrival sent a new mood of optimism coursing through the camp. On June the 24th this was enhanced by the wonderful news that Nicholson had routed 6000 rebels, sent to intercept the siege-train, at Najafgarh. 'I wish I had the power of knighting you on the spot,' Lawrence wrote. 'I hope you destroyed no end of villainous pandies.' He was somewhat taken aback when Nicholson confided his little scheme to start a mutiny of his own. Should General Wilson order a withdrawal from the city, Nicholson planned to appeal to the army to set him aside and elect a successor. Lawrence knew Delhi well and advised Nicholson to storm it at the Kashmir Gate, which is exactly what Nicholson did. The fact that he died nearby was very much his own rather than Lawrence's fault, since he insisted in leading a charge up a laneway against impossible odds, a piece of bravado which cost other lives as well. Lawrence was not surprised to hear that, on his deathbed, Nicholson thanked God that he still had the strength to 'shoot Wilson' if necessary.

By September the 21st Delhi was in British hands. Lawrence attempted, with no great success, to restrain the massacres which the troops visited upon the population by way of retribution. Throughout the length and breadth of the Empire he was proclaimed 'The Saviour of India'.

'Memorandum on the elimination of all Unchristian Principles from the Government of British India' was the title of a thought-provoking work published, in the aftermath of the crisis, by Herbert Edwards (who later wrote the inscription for the Nicholson Memorial). He attributed blame for the mutiny to, among other things, the secular tone of the Company's rule. Had the Bible featured in the curricula of the government schools, Sepoys might not have conceived the idea that they were to be duped into conversion to Christianity by contact with greased cartridges and bullock-bone flour. Thomas Arnold, Chief of the Punjab Education Department, challenged this proposal to introduce the Bible into the classrooms on the ground that the English were trustees of the Hindu. John Lawrence, in turn, contradicted Arnold. Arnold's position was based, he said, upon the assumption that 'the British government stood in the same relation towards the people of India as a representative government stands towards its people … If, by being trustees for the people, we are supposed to be bound by the will of the people, then we are not, the Chief-Commissioner thinks, trustees in that sense. We have not been elected or placed in power by the people, but we are here through our moral superiority by the force of circumstances, by the will of Providence. This alone constitutes our charter to govern India.'

England gave Lawrence a tremendous reception. The East India Company granted him a pension of £2000. London granted him the freedom of the city. The government made him a Baronet and Privy Councillor. Oxford and Cambridge awarded him honorary degrees. The Bishop of London praised his Christian principles. Herbert Edwards called him, among other things, 'a genuine Englishman'. The Queen and Prince Consort received him at Windsor. The same Lord Palmerston who had refused his father's pension entitlement now offered John the Viceroyalty of India. He became the first non-peer to hold the office.

By common consent his Raj was one of quiet progress. In Orissa one million people died of famine but that was the direct responsibility of the Lieutenant-Governor of Bengal rather than the Viceroy. A boom in Indian cotton was created by the American Civil War. When it was over, several banks crashed on account of the activities of speculators. Four out of five of his budgets showed deficits. He proposed to pay for new army barracks and new railways with a tax on income. This attracted virulent abuse. He was criticized for not adopting the manners of his aristocratic predecessors, for walking about unattended, for receiving a delegation of Calcutta dignitaries in his slippers, for retaining his old habit of rolling up his sleeves when working, for not being lavish enough as a host. But everyone agreed that, for pomp and splendour, his durbars at Lahore, Agra and Lucknow surpassed anything his predecessors had managed.

When, in the summer of 1867, the Lucknow Durbar was over, Lawrence stood alone in the room in the Residence where Henry had received the fatal shot.

And then he stood alone, in the garden of the Residence, by his brother's grave.

TWELVE

FOLEY'S STEP-GRANDFATHER, Benjamin Schrowder, came to Dublin from Winchelsea to work on the Custom House. Like many of the craftsmen who worked on the great project, he lived in the vicinity of the building, in Montgomery Street, now called Foley Street. He set up a workshop in the house he owned there, number 6, and stayed on after the Custom House was finished, having established a small business. He expected to return home one day, perhaps. But his children died in Dublin, then his wife Lavinia. All were buried in the churchyard at St George's at the top of Temple Street, not far from his house. Schrowder was heartbroken. He couldn't bear to leave the neighbourhood for any length of time. A relative told him of an aunt who was dying in Winchelsea, who owned a lot of property there. She intended to bequeath her fortune to

Benjamin, but he must visit her before it was too late to make sure of the inheritance. Schrowder wouldn't leave Dublin. And so he missed the bulk of the estate, although he did collect a few properties ... He carved the heads of the river gods which adorn the bridges over the Liffey, the most famous of which is that on O'Connell Bridge, a short distance from the O'Connell monument, upon which Foley spent the last ounces of his strength. He had planned to return from London, but he never made it. His final work straddles the boundary of his native parish.

When Lavinia died, Schrowder married a widow, Mrs Byrne. Her daughter Eliza married Jesse Foley, a glass-blower from Winchester, who later owned a grocer's shop in Mecklenburgh Street, now Sean MacDermott Street, around the corner from Montgomery Street. They had many children and lived under Schrowder's roof.

Edward, the elder boy, learned carving from Benjamin before becoming apprenticed to John Smith, master of the Dublin Society school.

Jesse and Eliza kept their children at home rather than send them to school. One room in the house was set aside for the classes conducted by Eliza. John Henry quickly became the bane of his mother's life on account of his fail-ure to concentrate on his lessons. The strong arm of Jesse was regularly summoned to administer correction. Agnes sometimes did her younger brother's addition and sub-traction to save him from their father's anger.

What John Henry enjoyed was to ramble off into the countryside beyond Ballybough by himself or with friends like J.J. McCarthy. They would climb trees, explore ditches and farmyards, join in football matches and fights, and hunt with troops of farming boys. They'd return home covered in muck, ravenously hungry and happy as larks. His mother and sisters doted upon young Foley. He was a little charmer. If he had a favourite among his sisters it was Martha, a year younger than himself, whose broken dolls he never tired of mending.

When Foley died, *The Times* reported that there were several ladies at his funeral, many of who laid wreaths upon his coffin, which was lowered through an opening in the pavement of St Paul's which had been covered by a black cloth.

On St Stephen's Day 1830, when he was aged twelve, Foley and J.J. were brought to the Dublin Society's premises in Merrion Square for an outing. There they saw a reproduction of the Apollo Belvedere, the masterpiece of Leochares.

'This is the sort of thing I'll spend my life at,' Foley announced to J.J.

He became serious. Where once he had been impossible to keep in the house, now no one could get him out of it. When J.J. called to Montgomery Street with a view to a spot of bird-nesting in Drumcondra or a swim on the North Strand, more often than not it was to be greeted by the cold shoulder of indifference, Foley not wanting to be disturbed from his book. He had started to read in earnest, making up for lost time.

Jesse Foley was not the man to permit any old rubbish to pervert the minds of his children. The only novel allowed into the house was *The Vicar of Wakefield*, a copy of which Foley would keep by him all his life. He read and re-read Young's *Night Thoughts* and *Hervey's Meditations*. The bar on newspapers was absolute.

Foley began to display an active interest in the daily concerns of the household, particularly at the level of repairing things. Windows, chairs, tables, banisters, toys – nothing was useless for long. Not content with that, he began to make things from scratch: cups, beakers, vessels of all kinds. He hammered together a bench for the younger children's use in the classroom.

Jesse was secretly delighted, of course, believing that he had effected the transformation by judicious use of the strap.

Mrs Foley was as astonished as she was delighted and started to think out loud about apprenticing him to a carpenter or an upholsterer.

'If my mother said she intends to do this she'll surely do it,' Foley confided to Martha. 'But I'll run away.'

Happily it never came to that. Foley was entered instead into the Art Schools of the Dublin Society where he quickly established himself as the outstanding pupil. Every day he walked to the school, entering via the Kildare Street gate early in the morning and leaving late in the evening.

Is it fanciful to imagine the paths of Foley and the youthful John Nicholson crossing in the Dublin of the 1830s? How could the arts student have guessed that the little boy he saw playing soldiers in St Stephen's Green was destined, thirty years later, to become his subject?

One evening, just before an examination, Foley returned to Montgomery Street under a cloud. He related to his mother how a malicious classmate had broken the model he was due to submit for assessment the following day. Distraught, Eliza proposed to report the matter to the appropriate authorities the following day. Foley, however, had other ideas.

'Mother, do you have any candles?' he enquired.

'I do indeed, but why ever do you want them, John?'

'I am going to hide in the college tonight and remake my model!'

And he set off once more, a determined little figure, with the candles concealed under his jacket. That evening, as the porter locked the door, Foley hid behind a pillar in the hallway. Suddenly he was enshrouded in darkness. He waited five minutes, then lit his candle.

The shadow of the Apollo Belvedere moved along the wall.

Foley held his candle beneath the head, then passed it along the outstretched arm, following the intricate movement of the cloak under the left shoulder and back across the elbow. So natural, so breathtaking.

'Into the studio!' Apollo seemed to say. 'Model!'

Foley's audacity bore fruit. To the dismay of the miscreant who had smashed his original effort, he submitted a superior model to his examiners the following day. He won four prizes: in modelling, architectural drawing, studies of the human form, ornamental design. It was an unprecedented achievement.

Edward was by now established in London at the workshop of Mr Behnes. He persuaded the family that John Henry must join him there to enrol in the school of the Royal Academy. The Foley girls were distraught at the prospect of losing their second darling to the big city so soon after the first.

'Now don't cry,' said he. 'I'll be a great man some day. I'll buy you a silk dress.'

Foley arrived in the metropolis in March of 1834 and at first devoted himself exclusively to sculpture. His early work, *The Death of Abel*, won for him a studentship at the Academy for ten years. Now he felt it wise to broaden his horizons somewhat and he took up the study of music and poetry as well. He sent verses to his mother and a song entitled 'Past and Present', a reflection on the contrast between his old circumstances and the new.

At the age of twenty he suffered an attack of jaundice, brought about by overwork. He was given bad medical advice. He should immediately have adopted a diet of the most nourishing food possible, but instead he was put on a very low diet. Although he recovered eventually, the result of this treatment was that his complexion lost its clear red and white tones and became somewhat swarthy. Everyone in Montgomery Street was dismayed to hear about this, although of course they were relieved that he had recovered.

Edward gained his brother an entrée to Behnes' workshop, nursery of some of the finest sculptors of the day, like John Thomas and Leuthwaite Watson. Apart from developing his craft under Behnes' expert guidance, Foley also picked up other skills a sculptor needed to acquire if he was to have a successful career.

Chief among these was sociability. Visiting artists' studios was a popular pastime of ladies and gentlemen of the day. For the apprentice these occasions were an opportunity to meet people and develop the contacts that ought in time to lead to commissions. Foley quickly spotted that it would be as well for him to extend his general education parallel to his sculpting skills, since few people stayed interested for long in a man who could only speak of carving.

He bounced back from the jaundice problem with typical elan. In 1839, his *Death of Abel* and *Innocence* were exhibited at the Royal Academy to tremendous acclaim. In the latter work, a twelve-year-old girl in ancient Greek costume holding a dove against her shoulder, Edward saw a portrait of Martha. So far as we know, he made no such family connection in respect of the former piece, for the two brothers were always on excellent terms. The following year *Ino and Bacchus* was exhibited to further acclaim. This was typical of Foley, to move from the subject of innocence to the infant god of wine and his mother. He lies on his back, grinning, reaching for the bunch of grapes dangled above him by the bare-breasted mother who lies smiling by his side. The naturalness, charm and wit of the piece affected all who saw it, especially the Earl of Ellesmere, who ordered a copy in marble for his gallery at Bridgewater House.

Ino's breasts are not large, but neither are they small. They are pleasant but, from a sculpting point of view, unremarkable items. *Innocence* of course has no breasts at all.

The success placed Foley in the top flight of sculptors at the tender age of twenty-two. *The Art Journal* now began to champion his cause, publishing the first of a series of engravings and reviews of his work. Edward married the love of his life, the daughter of Mr Smith, his old Dublin master, so John Henry moved in with a fellow artist to new premises on Hampstead Road. *The Death of Lear* and *The Homeless Wanderer* won the Academicians' praise in 1841 and 1842, but it was with *The Youth at the Stream* in the following year that Foley fulfilled the expectations raised by *Ino and Bacchus*. The youth wears a fig leaf in the manner of the Apollo Belvedere, and holds his right arm vertically above to grasp the branch of a tree, as he tests the water with his foot. There was an inscription:

> *Playful and wanton to the stream he trips*
> *and dips his foot.*

Edward recognized in this work the spirit of his brother's wanderings in the fields near Ballybough. *The Art Union* journal declared that 'if this had been dug up in Rome or Naples, mutilated, it would have been pronounced a valuable specimen of classic art'.

Now Foley approached the next great test of his career. St Stephen's Hall in the new houses of Parliament at Westminster was designed to accommodate marble statues of outstanding figures from the history of the great institution. An open competition was organized, with a view to commissioning work from the winners. Every sculptor in England submitted work. Foley was represented by his *Youth* and *Ino and Bacchus*. He, Bell and Marshall were the three artists commissioned from the event, with John Henry getting John Hampden and Selden.

Hampden was exhibited in 1847, again to acclaim. Every neo-classical sculpture may be regarded as an interplay between ideal and realistic elements. Hampden was acknowledged a wonderful synthesis of both. The seventeenth-century clothes are represented with vitality and painstaking accuracy, from the patterned lace collar around his neck to the leather riding boots whose tops droop about his knees. His right hand rests upon the hilt of his sword, the tip of which touches the ground. The left has gathered his cloak, together with a scroll of paper, up to his chest. His head is erect, gaze straight ahead, as if he were about to address an audience. Gestures and posture were considered to embody wonderfully well the qualities of resolution and courtesy for which Hampden was renowned. From the long-term point of view, the clothes were more significant, for it was in this aspect of his work that Foley was later considered to have developed an individual style which heralded the triumph of naturalism in the years that followed his death.

Hampden earned many commissions for Foley. His name became known outside the artistic circles in which it was already celebrated. Members of the royal family acquired his work. In short, he became famous. He married. He moved to new premises in London's Osnaburgh Street, destined to be his home and workplace for more than twenty years. All that remained to complete the young man's happiness was that his mother should come to live with him, Jesse Foley having died some time before.

A room for Eliza was prepared in Osnaburgh Street, a great armchair installed at the fireside, and then he sent for her – only to receive a summons to Dublin, an urgent one. She was dying. The Foley brothers wasted not a moment before rushing home, but they were too late. She passed away just as their boots clattered around the corner of Montgomery Street.

How much of Eliza returned to earth in *The Mother*, which he carved soon afterwards? Who now can judge if the young woman – who in truth smacks more of Mount Olympus than Montgomery Street – has a likeness of Eliza Schrowder Byrne? Save for a drape fallen about her hips and thighs, she is naked. She lies on her side and gazes – fondly, intelligently, reflectively – at the curly-headed children, girl and boy, who play beside her as she reclines. This was Foley's riposte to death. He summoned up Eliza's spirit and breathed it into the stone where it might remain forever.

The mother's breasts are slightly larger than Ino's, but it's difficult to imagine them suckling the children.

Was Foley thinking of Edward when he carved *The Elder Brother from Comus?* It looks like the Apollo Belvedere in a different pose. The fig leaf perches on the groin. The cloak hangs loosely across the left wrist and forearm. He's upright, stepping boldly forward. This is a brave brother, a pathfinder, like the one who dared to fall in love with his master's daughter and made a tour of the studios of London at sixteen, asking to carve marble, and who was prepared to go to Rome to work if necessary, but who found a place in the best studio in the city. Since Foley's practice was to understand the essence of a subject before he set to work, surely he had only to contemplate Edward for this piece, which required that he must consider brotherliness? He could not have forseen Edward's suicide, a few months before his own death.

And of whom did he think, if anyone, when he modelled *Egeria*, the goddess who fell in love with Numa, the Roman king, which served as the companion piece for *The Elder Brother* in the Egyptian Room at the Mansion House in London – Edward's wife? His own? The cloth flows around her wonderfully rounded hips as she stands against a rock, resting her hand upon the stump of a tree, pulling her hair away from her ear with her right hand …

Here didst thou dwell in this enchanted cover
Egeria! thy all heavenly bosom beating
For the far footsteps of thy mortal lover.

Here, the goddess's breasts are a slight billowing from her chest.

Foley exhibited every year at the Academy throughout the 1850s. His next sensation, *Viscount Hardinge*, was displayed in front of Burlington House prior to its departure for India. This won rapturous acclaim, and Foley was deeply proud of the fact that his fellow artists tried to raise money to keep a copy in England. They ranked it with the great equestrian statues of Europe – *Marcus Aurelius* on the Capitol in Rome, Donatello's *Gattamelata* in the Piazza San Antonio in Padua, Verocchio's bronze *Coleoni* in Venice, Rauch's *Friedrich the Great* in Berlin.

What thrilled was the sheer vitality of the horse. *The Art Journal* described it as 'bold, almost daring, in conception, and masterly in execution', the noblest equestrian statue of modern times. It reported that, in Calcutta, the 'Arab horse dealers, with whom the love of the horse is a passion, and knowledge of their points of excellence a universal acquirement, are daily to be seen gazing at it. A more impressive admiration than that of these wild children of the desert, it is impossible to witness anywhere.'

The Queen made Foley's acquaintance. She was to visit his studio on two occasions. When the time came to cast Gough, Foley thought it would be a good idea to use metal melted from guns he'd captured from the Chinese and the Sikhs. Parliament offered a prayer to the sovereign for this and Victoria granted the request.

Although he was much sought after in society, Foley declined more invitations than he accepted. When he did attend a social gathering he invariably left early, otherwise 'he could not do the work he was obliged to do tomorrow'. The one occasion on which Foley could be relied upon to down tools was when friends from Ireland were due to visit. He would instruct his wife to purchase 'great big joints – that is what they like'. Anything left over was given to the poor after the night of feasting, fun and music.

He taught himself to play the flute. He composed songs. Often he would play to himself until the early hours of the morning. The names of these pieces, the words, the airs – all, with one exception, have vanished.

Foley and his wife had no children. Two of his sisters came to London to live with them. He loved young people and especially loved children's parties, at which he'd cut out animals from cardboard with a pen-knife for their amusement.

His studio was directly beside his home. At work, he wore a black silk cap and long grey coat. He was not given to much talking. He spent his time working on the various pieces under construction, supervising his apprentices and workmen. He had a gallery in which finished casts were arranged on either side, with a bust on a pedestal between each two figures. There were lines of workshops behind curtains where work was carried out upon the various pieces under construction. At the end of the gallery there was a space with a high ceiling for equestrian models. Since he kept his works until he was satisfied that absolutely nothing more was to be done with them, many remained at Osnaburgh Street for a long time. Sir James Outram was with him twelve years.

Visitors took delight in being conducted about the gallery by the sculptor himself. Some had the pleasure of being alone in his company at this time. Tenniswood, his pupil, recalled pacing through the workshop with him at night, inspecting each piece by the light of the lamp. Although their object was the practical one of determining how to advance the work on particular pieces the next day, there was a belief at the time that the best way to see sculpture, to savour the mysteries of stone and clay, was by the light of the lamp or the torch. The ancients had believed this, it was thought.

Foley's career was not all sweetness and light. There was the problem of Baron Marochetti. He, because he was Italian and well connected, his rivals thought, often was awarded plum commissions – even when he hadn't competed for them like everybody else. In 1854 Foley exhibited his design for a memorial to the Duke of Wellington: the Duke sheaths his sword having defeated the Spirit of War and elevated the Spirit of Peace – but the commission for the job went to the Baron, who had submitted nothing. Foley, however, got his own back later on, in the matter of the Albert Memorial in Hyde Park.

Now Foley had already completed three memorials for the Prince Consort who, in an age of heroes, was being promoted by his widow as the greatest hero of them all. One was in Birmingham, another in Cambridge, and the last was in Dublin. For the great national monument at Hyde Park, he had already been commissioned to produce one of the four groups representing the continents which were to be positioned at each corner of the monument. With typical courtesy, he let his colleagues have their choice of continent first, and accordingly was left with *Asia*, which the others considered to be something of an embarrassment on account of the elephant. Anyhow, the Baron got the plum, the production of Albert, the centrepiece. But his first effort was rejected as unsatisfactory, and so was his second, which he completed just before his death. The Queen herself insisted that Foley make his fourth Albert.

So Foley set to work on an enormous figure which, had it been standing, would have been nineteen feet tall. The Prince is seated on a throne, his head tilted forward so that it is positioned directly in the centre of the arch above when viewed from the side as well as from beneath, and also, as he explained to the committee, to show Albert taking an active rather than a passive interest in the works of civilization being conducted below him. The general idea was, as usual, to combine the realistic and the ideal.

A representation of Albert's physiognomy combined with an expression of his essential character – his high position in the world, his integrity, his humanity.

The purpose of the monument – which would bear the inscription 'Queen Victoria and her people' – was to celebrate the benefits advanced to mankind by Victoria's reign. At the base of the throne would be a frieze depicting all the wondrous achievements of the age. Then, at the four corners of the monument, the four continents, each represented by a woman, with the different racial sub-groups beneath her, represented by men, the peoples who received the benefits. There is an Indian warrior holding his sword, a Chinese craftsman holding a vase, a Persian poet holding a pen, an Arab holding the Koran.

Foley's practice was to study and contemplate the details of the lives of those who were his subjects before he made their shape, so that he could identify the essentials, the ideal quality he had to embody in the matter. So what was the quality of these people? What did they embody? How did they relate to each other? How did they relate to the Prince? Were they simply a representative gathering of racially inferior, conquered peoples, who ought to be glad of the possibility of improvement which contact with Britain afforded them? This was how Sir George Gilbert Scott, the designer of the monument, clearly perceived them.

Some art critics, including one or two who knew Foley and his work very well, took the view that Foley did not share this perception.

They noted that all the figures in the group have their backs turned to one another. In other words, they do not relate to one another at all. They refuse to acknowledge the relationship devised for them by Sir George Gilbert Scott. The Indian is looking in the general direction of the Albert Hall across the road; the Chinese, sitting cross-legged at the Indian's feet, seems to be in trance, perhaps induced by opium; on the other side of the group, the Persian poet stares at the heavens; the Arab, like the Chinese, is grounded, leaning against a camel-saddle. None are looking at Albert, or relating to any of the other figures on the crowded monument either for that matter. Some saw in this arrangement an expression of scorn on Foley's part for the subject, indeed an expression of defiance for the concept, which forced unnatural relationships upon things which were, in truth, quite independent of one another.

Had the iconographer of Hardinge and Canning, of Outram, Gough, Nicholson and many others, the conquerors of Asia, suffered a change of heart when it came to representing Asia? Was he suddenly conscious of a sudden loathing on his part for the Queen, her consort and all their works? Did he suddenly have a vision of himself as the mindless lackey and celebrant of imperialism, the enslavement of half the globe? Or did he simply follow his methods and procedures and carve what emerged, which is what he had always done?

What was he thinking of when he shaped the magnificent woman who sits upon the elephant?

This female is a far cry from *Egeria* or *Ino*, *Innocence* or *The Mother*. She is large, languid, sensuous, rich. There are jewels around her neck and arms, around her wrists, around her forehead. She is lifting a veil from her face, which is calm and proud and transcendentally beautiful. Her breasts are startlingly big and voluptuous.

This regal woman feigns no interest in the doings of the busy British people upon the frieze behind her. And the great crouching elephant upon which she sits is rather magnificent too, and so faithfully observed, with his curling trunk, wrinkled skin and mood of quiet, sullen potency.

Shaping the woman cost Foley his life. For he spent long hours sitting on the limbs of the figure, on wet clay, to model the bust. This brought on the attack of pleurisy which began the tedious process of his death.

Thus Asia wrought revenge on Foley.

Thus Foley sacrificed his life for an ideal.

The doctors wanted him to quit England entirely for the Mediterranean, but he could not bring himself to leave his studio and his workmen. He travelled only as far as Hastings, where he wrote the only poem of his which survives, his *envoi*, 'Here We Must Part'.

> *Farewell, forget me, may thy days roll on*
> *Still blessed, till time shall be no more.*
> *I would not have thy bosom harbour one*
> *Dark drop that sorrow from its depths might pour,*
> *Farewell, cast from thy glistening eyes*
> *Those tears, and let them be*
> *The last that evermore shall rise*
> *In memory of me.*

Most supposed this was addressed to his wife. But it might equally have been addressed to *Asia*.

His days were full of sadness, as he paced the gallery, contemplating in the workshops embryos whose birth he would not see. He prepared to pass the mantle to the chosen ones among his disciples, Tenniswood and Brock.

Foley concentrated his penultimate effort on *Albert*, and his final effort on *Daniel O'Connell*. Erin leads a troop of her countrymen, beneficiaries of Emancipation won by O'Connell, points upwards to the Liberator above her, clutching in her hand a scroll inscribed with his favourite poem:

> *Oh, where's the slave so lowly*
> *condemn'd to chains unholy*
> *Who, could he burst*
> *His bonds at first*
> *Would pine beneath them slowly?*

He had the model complete when, on the 6th of August, 1874, an attack of pleuritic effusion began in his new home in Hampstead, where he had moved for the country air. Three weeks later Foley died.

When Sir George Gilbert Scott was casting about for a design for the memorial for Albert, he hit upon the old Germanic idea of a Valhalla. Why not build such a place for the prince? It was objected that London already had two Valhallas, one the cathedral at Westminster, the other that at St Paul's. There Foley was taken, to lie with Nelson and Wellington, Herbert Edwardes, John Moore, Robert Montgomery and other members of the heavenly comitatus.

THIRTEEN

I WAS DRAWN back to the story my mother had told me when she was ironing. Which meant going back to India, to Calcutta, to the Maidan, to join the family and Colonel Blenkinsop *en route* to the picnic he had arranged as a peace offering following the destruction of his greenhouse.

I stole a car outside an office in Dalhousie Square. I drove to Fort William, where I collected Rita and Francisco from their hotel. Rita wore henna in her hair and a sari. She murmured in Hindi to Francisco, who sported the turban of a Sikh, white cotton jacket and trousers. Next we picked up Stephen, Babington and Lally from a restaurant near Hoogly, all of them sweating profusely in their cotton suits.

The Maidan was teeming with people. Towering above them, three great Foley equestrian statues: Canning, Hardinge, Outram.

I caught a glimpse of them by the Hardinge statue. The little girls in their white muslin dresses and broad-brimmed straw hats. And there was my grandfather. The emotion I had nourished for him welled up inside me. Longing. Sheer longing. And I could not speak to him. Because my heart was broken.

I wanted to say Grandfather! It's me! I've come to save you. Don't go on the picnic with Blenkinsop!

Then we spotted Colonel Blenkinsop, striding the Maidan to meet them. I accelerated slightly, scattering the crowd.

My impulse was to collar him and carve him. Bring him to a studio and carve him. So that his image would be fixed forever by my knife.

Rita slipped out of the car, carrying a suitcase. She approached Colonel Blenkinsop and, in a mixture of English and Hindi, asked him for assistance. In seconds, he was carrying her suitcase for her and placing it at the base of the Hardinge statue.

Meanwhile, Stephen and Francisco were placing suitcases at the foot of the Canning statue. And Lally and Babington suitcases at the foot of the Outram statue.

Three little girls and their mother were at the door of my car. 'Are you going on the picnic?' I asked. 'Come on. I'll give you a lift.'

'We're with the Colonel. Are you with the Colonel's party?'

'Oh yes. I know the Colonel.'

'Well thank you. That's very kind of you. Get in girls – it's Mamie, Georgina, Patricia. I'll just fetch my husband.'

We were coasting along the Barrackpur Road, in dizzy sweltering silence, when the first explosion sounded.

SOURCES AND ACKNOWLEDGMENTS

The following are quotes unattributed in the text:

Page 23, 'Chillianwallah, Chillianwallah ...', George Meredith; page 32, 'Who has not heard ...', *Lalla Rookh – An Oriental Romance*, Thomas Moore; page 33, 'There's a bower of roses ...', *ibid.*; page 50, 'A day of onsets ...', Alfred, Lord Tennyson; page 51, 'I met with murder ...', Percy Bysshe Shelley; page 53, 'O, pardon me ...', *Julius Caesar*, Act III, Part I; page 60, 'Lead out the pageant ...', 'Ode on the Death of the Duke of Wellington', Alfred, Lord Tennyson; page 87, 'Ye who have joyed to read ...', 'The Bayard of India', Anon.; page 99, 'Banner of England ...', Alfred, Lord Tennyson; page 100, 'Hark cannode ...', 'The Siege of Lucknow', Alfred, Lord Tennyson; page 128, 'Here didst thou dwell ...', *Childe Harold*, Canto IV, Stanza 118, George Gordon, Lord Byron; page 136, 'Oh, where's the slave ...', Thomas Moore.

These books have provided a background for *Foley's Asia*:

Sarah Atkinson, *John Henry Foley* (Dublin 1882); F.P. Gibbon, *The Lawrences of the Punjab* (London 1908); Charles Hardinge, *Rulers of India* (Oxford 1891); William C. Monkhouse, *The Works of John Henry Foley* (Spalding 1875); J.L. Morrison, *Lawrence of Lucknow* (London 1905); Robert S. Rait, *Life and Campaigns of Hugh First Viscount Gough* (London 1903); Lionel Trotter, *The Life of John Nicholson* (London 1898) and *The Life of John Outram* (Edinburgh 1903); Charles Wogan, *Female Fortitude ... the seizure, escape and marriage of the Princess Clementine Sobieski* (London 1722).

Many people and institutions helped me in the writing of this book. They include: my mother, Georgiana Adye-Curran, who told me her childhood memories of India; my friend Brendan Walsh, who told me his memories of Dublin; my friend Robert Maharry; my brother Jeremiah Sheehan; the Cosgrave brothers, Peter, Joe, Michael, and their father Jack; in Derry, Kitty O'Kane; Claire D'Arcy; Carol Foster; my son, Luke Sheehan; An Chomhairle Ealaíon; the staff of The Princess Grace Irish Library, Monaco; the staff of the Bibliothèque Municipale, Nice; the staff of the National Library, Dublin.